Jean-Claude Racinet

ANOTHER HORSEMANSHIP

A manual of riding in the French Classical tradition.

XENOPHON PRESS

CONTENTS

PART FOUR

"NO-NO's"

CONCLUSION

INTRODUCTION

This being a short book — a practical manual — I have limited my talk to describing the horsemanship of French Tradition from a down-to-earth point of view. I, therefore, think I owe my readers some general considerations on the subject by way of an introduction.

The French style is characterized by lightness.

Of course, I do not pretend that the French have the monopoly on lightness, since there have been Frenchmen who did not abide by its philosophy (all the more so nowadays, when lightness does not feature as a condition for a good ranking in modern Dressage competitions), and since there have been many non-French riders who cherished lightness.

In the course of history, horsemanship has evolved much. Baroque riding, for instance (the 17th and 18th centuries), is not at all what well-intended idealists would like it to have been; horses were overly poised onto their hocks, they rarely were going straight (two track movements were the rule) and, even when they were going straight, they were kept in a "pli" (a lateral bending) that was supposed to be indispensable to any good presentation at the time. Flying changes of lead at a canter were, if not unheard of, at least considered as an uninteresting stunt; bits and spurs were still dreadful, etc.

François Baucher (1796-1873) reacted against these exaggeratedly restrained airs of the Baroque style, and we owe him our modern optic of horses performing in a more "horizontal" balance, allowing "tempi" flying changes up to flying changes of lead at every stride, which he is the first to have performed currently with all his horses.

For circumstantial reasons which would be too long to consider here, but have much more to do with politics and national pride than with technical necessities, the Germans have never acknowledged Baucher (although they have followed an evolution that he was the beacon of). They cling, verbally at least, to La Guérinière (another Frenchman, by the way).

François Robichon de La Guérinière (1688-1751) is considered as the best theorist of the "baroque" horsemanship, because of the importance and quality of his book *Ecole de Cavalerie* first published in 1731 (although many books were published in the 18th century by other very distinguished riders, who did not all adhere to La Guérinière's way). As it happens, La Guérinière is the inventor of "shoulder-in," a movement which has undergone many vicissitudes and is nowadays generally practiced and taught in a way quite different from La Guérinière's.

La Guérinière is also the first to have described (and advocated as "one of the most refined aids of horsemanship") the practice of "release of the hand," by which a horse is left in "liberty on parole" after he has been set in the proper balance.

Baucher's main book's title, *Methode d'équitation basée sur de nouveaux principes* ("Method of Horsemanship Based on New Principles," 1842) expresses his desire to be an innovator, but in a field like that of horsemanship, it is almost impossible to start from scratch. "Half-halts" are not his invention, nor is "lateral work" ("two-track movements"). His way to teach a horse how to back up resembles much to this of La Guérinière's; and, although he had declared proudly that before him "nobody had understood anything to the problem of collection," he ended up practicing a collection which evokes much that of the baroque era, but perfected since the rear end of the horse was no longer crushed and overly bent.

In the perspective view of History, it appears that the main discovery of Baucher's is the seeking to lightness of the jaw as a prerequisite to any movement, through "flexions of the jaw."

His philosophy, which can hardly be discarded, is that no movement whatsoever should be asked for as long as the conditions of balance required by its execution have not been realized. Hence, "never ask at fast gaits what you cannot get at slow ones," and create first the balance by which means is the most appropriate, half-halt or yielding of the jaw (this latter generating an altogether state of relaxation with the horse).

Determining as they might have been, Baucher's innovations appear more as improvements — very important ones — grafted onto classical knowledge, than as a denial of this very knowledge. And it appears to me that the evolution of the French riding is characterized by a constant seeking toward more lightness, with Baucher in his second style (1864) as its more exquisite theorist and practitioner. If, for instance, we limit ourselves to taking only *one* item from both great French equerries, the "shoulder-in" from La Guérinière and the "yielding of the jaw" from Baucher, we are already going to train our horses wonderfully and achieve magnificent results in High School riding. Let us note, incidentally, that neither of the two above mentioned items are present in the modern — German-like — Dressage riding; shoulder-in is reduced to some kind of subliminal lateral movement, with the bending exhibiting mainly — not to say merely — in the front end of the horse, and yielding of the jaw discarded as placing the horse "behind the bit" (an expression which has done much harm to horsemanship).

This "French-like" horsemanship grafting the Baucherist procedures (lateral and direct flexions of the neck and poll from the ground and, when mounted, at slow paces; maintenance of a permanent yielding of the jaw in action; "effet d'ensemble" followed with a total release of the aids; sophistication in the use of the spurs; work in place; importance bestowed upon the movement of rein back...) to the classical progression of La Guérinière (circle; shoulder-in, croup to the wall) is, as it happens, the horsemanship practiced in a very recent past by the unforgettable Portuguese Master, Nuno Oliveira.

Then in full possession of his Art, Oliveira was first spotted by a group of French riders touring Portugal in the 1950's. Amazed by his "Maestria," they asked, "What kind of horsemanship is this marvelous one that you practice?" And, equally stunned, Oliveira stuttered, "But...yours, of course; the Traditional French Horsemanship."

For it is another tragedy of our time that even the French have forsaken their own heritage.

But let us, for a moment, forget France and Germany, La Guérinière and Baucher, the present and the past, Dressage competitive riding and High School artistic riding.

The gist of the question lies in a simple choice:

On the one hand, a permanent, simultaneous and often forceful wielding of the aids, in order to make the horse accept a rather firm contact with the bit.

On the other hand, the seeking to lightness through an alternate, delicate wielding of the aids, meant at leaving the horse as soon and as often as possible in "liberty on parole."

The first way offers an undisputable advantage: you won't fall from the horse, since reins rarely break. But you will obtain only a mediocre balance and, even with the best of horses, your performances will look "heavy," your pirouettes will be lazy, your passage miserable. And, at a piaffe, you will happen to piaffe yourself more than your horse.

The second will give you undescribable joy, and will allow you to teach any horse some High School movements.

The author, Tunis, 1956.

PART ONE

Change Your Riding Habits

I. Quit Pushing Onto the Bit

When one pushes a horse with the legs, he goes forward, and so does the bit. So, not much should happen as concerns the coming "onto the bit" of the horse, unless one pushes and pulls at the same time.

Now, if you push and pull together you give your horse two opposite orders: "go--don't go," and he can only be confused by the contradiction. Most of the time, he will choose to obey only one of these two orders--the one that fits best his character. All you're going to get is a dull horse who will respond with less and less generosity to your legs' orders. Or, if the horse decides to obey your legs, he will have to put up with your hands' traction and will become heavier and heavier on the bit.

Or both.

II. "Hand Without Legs, Legs Without Hand"
(Separation of the aids)

Legs Without Hand

If, by contrast, you *systematically open your fingers* as you give an impulsive order with your legs, your horse will feel free, and will be more inclined to obey. This suppresses a major obstacle to impulsion.

This does not mean that you are going to "abandon" your horse on the forehand, for as soon as he will have started, you are justified in controlling his pace with your hands, if necessary. It just means that, as you started, you did not press down two pedals together--the accelerator and the brake.

It is better to open your fingers than to move your hand forward. By opening your fingers, you kind of drop the reins, though they still remain in your hands, so at any time, you can clench your fingers on them in order to control the movement, if necessary. There should be *no opposition whatsoever* to the horse's stretching his neck as he starts the movement. If he feels you are going to restrict him, he won't go freely. Horses are very sensitive; they know if your fingers are going to be "permissive" or not.

Most riders establish their balance off the reins, not only for lack of a good seat, but also out of an unconscious fear. Now, if you content yourself with moving your hands forward when you "yield," you kind of cheat, for you are loath to release your grip on the reins, and the horse knows it. So, *do open the fingers*. Ask a friend to check on you in the beginning. Old reflexes (of clenching the reins as one uses the legs) are stubborn.

Exercises

1) Halt. Drop the reins completely (don't even touch them). Ask for a walk with your legs, and grab and adjust your reins as soon as you walk. You may be very fast in grabbing the reins, but you must do that only after the walk has started.

2) Walk. Drop the reins completely (don't even touch them). Ask for a trot with your legs, and grab and adjust your reins as you trot, but *not before*.

3) (If you have enough guts. As a matter of fact, it is very easy, but it is impressive.) Halt. Drop your reins completely (don't even touch them). With your legs, ask for a canter. Take your reins only as you canter, but not before. (For the way to use your legs for this exercise, see Part Two, Section III; **Legs**).

These exercises are meant to get rid of the habit people have of pulling on the reins while simultaneously using their legs.

As a rule, the rider must learn how to be "nimble" with his hands, let the reins slide easily, then readjust them in a jiffy (see Part Two, Section II; **Hands**). A constant, discrete, but efficient readjustment of the rein is a "must," for the horse should never feel "locked in," as he nevertheless ought to be controlled.

[2]

All riders are taught to slow or stop a horse by opposing their seat and legs to their hands, in order to keep the horse "engaged." This comes from the time when horses were schooled between the pillars. Since they could not move forward, they rapidly learned how to "cower" upon the slightest impulsive demand. So the legs of the rider had an engaging effect, when they were opposed to the checking action of the hand.

As a counterpart, when the matter was to really go forward, the riders were obliged to use dire spurs, for their legs had taken a somewhat negative, slowing down meaning.

But nowadays, with our horses, the addition of the legs' action to any checking order with the hand, will needlessly complicate the horse's task. One more time: "Go—don't." Or rather, this time: "don't go—go."

To slow or stop a horse with the mere hand, you have to apply specific actions (see Part Two, Section II).

III. Release of the Aids

A rider should not accept that his/her aids not be obeyed immediately; that is to say, they should rapidly bring about some kind of *transformation* in the horse's gait, speed, movement, or balance.

Everybody will agree on that.

Very few, though, will think of the corollary which is when the aid has brought about the desired transformation, *IT MUST QUIT*. If it does not, if it lasts, it denies its value as a means of transformation; it self-depreciates.

In other words, if you push, push, push with your legs, although there is no acceleration, you literally program your horse according to the formula: "My legs mean NOTHING, my legs mean NOTHING, my legs mean NOTHING."

Your legs mean acceleration, so when you have reached the speed you wanted to get, they have to quit. If they don't either the horse will go on accelerating, and you will have exceeded your own intention, or he will quit accelerating although your legs are still on, and you will blunt their power.

The same with the hands. Your hands mean deceleration. When your horse slows down to the point you want, *stop your hand action*.

Of course, in the beginning at least, your horse will slow after you've

[3]

opened your legs, or he will accelerate after you have opened your fingers. So wield your aids again in order to restore the situation, and then *disengage them*. Be patient. Be stubborn. In time your horse will learn that *he* (and not you) has to maintain the speed, gait, movement, etc. where he has been placed by *your* action.

Self-impulsion (through systematic release of legs) and self-carriage (through systematic release of hand) will be your reward. Then, little by little, as collection builds up, you will obtain self-collection. Your aids, disengaged as the horse maintains, from his own will, impulsion, balance, and collection, will be free for more interesting tasks: piaffe, passage, canter pirouettes, and tempi flying changes will become easy. You will enter the realm of High School.

Remember:

1) Your aids should never be ignored by the horse;

2) They should *always* be disengaged upon completion of the order, so that...

3) As long as there is no need for a transformation (transition), you must ride free wheel.

Said differently: Your aids should never be used to maintain a speed, gait, etc.; they should bring them about or restore them. If a steady action of the aids accompanies a steady speed, gait, etc., you've headed for heaviness.

In the beginning, ask a friend to yell at you when you wind up pushing for nothing. Old reflexes are hard to forget.

Last, but not least: quit wiggling in the saddle. You must also practice release of seat.

IV. Moderation of the Aids

Riding literature is full of expressions like "energetic actions of the legs," or "graduated action of the legs," inferring that there is a proportional relation between the strength of the action of the rider's legs and the energy and vivacity of the horse's response. This is a misconception. If it were true, jockeys would ride with long stirrups and would attend body building courses.

Horses were not born with little accelerators in the ribs so that they run when you press them. It's quite the opposite; when you use your legs for the first time on a horse who has never been ridden before, he tends to slow down or stop and, sometimes, tries to bite the rider's boot!

[4]

So the rider's leg will draw all its impulsive power from a conditioning. After the horse has been given this specific conditioning (see Part Two, Section III), he is never to forget it, *if* the riding has been correct (that is, applying the principles of release, separation, and moderation of aids). But, if he should forget, a stronger action of leg would be to no avail for it would not address the real problem, which is that he forgot the meaning of the leg action. What ought to be done then is to "refresh" the conditioning.

Apply this situation to yourself: If I speak to you in Greek and you do not understand me because you do not speak Greek, will you understand better if I *SHOUT?*

Either the horse "speaks legs" or he doesn't. If he does, it is useless to shout. And if he does not, it is stupid.

So you must limit the strength of your leg actions to the minimum he can feel, which is the standard action he has to become obedient to, through the specific conditioning we have already mentioned.

The action of hand does not follow the same pattern. It may be very strong occasionally, but it should never last more than one-half second. In other words, the action should be "pulsated" ("take and give").

This is explained by the phenomenon of "action and reaction," which applied as much in the psychological domain as it does in the physical one. The action of the rider's hand *always* provokes a reaction from the horse's neck, in the other direction. Fortunately, there is a slight time lag between this reaction and the action which brought it about, so one may expect that, if the action of hand is short enough, the reaction from the horse will not come about.

So, whichever result an action of hand has brought about in this determining half-second, it must then cease. Would it last longer, the overall result would be lesser, for there would be a fight between the rider's hand and the horse's mouth. Avoiding this fight will give the hand action its optimal value.

Of course, this short, but occasionally powerful, action of hand will be repeated until the desired result is obtained.

Remember:

Only one action of the hands that lasts *too long* will create contractions with the horse, and bring about a mediocre result. A "pulsated" action of the hand will relax the horse and bring about a fast result.

To sum it up, the principle of moderation of aids states that the aids should never exceed a given threshold: of STRENGTH for the legs; of

DURATION for the hands.

The old reflexes to forget are:

1) To come stronger with the legs or to kick with the heels, in the event the horse ignores the legs (instead of immediately adding the action of the crop).

2) To resist with the hands for more than one-half second.

Have somebody check on you, for your good will alone won't suffice to erase these wrong reflexes.

V. Optimization of Orders

If your handwriting is bad, you won't improve it by writing books. You must break down the difficulty, form separate letters first, then try series of letters, etc.

If your horse does not canter correctly, you won't improve it by cantering tirelessly. For one, how could he understand? There is no such thing as a "bad" or a "good" canter, for a horse's mind; he just gives you the *ONLY* canter he can produce given his condition of balance of the moment.

BALANCE is the master word.

Establish the balance first, then ask for a canter. As soon as the canter deteriorates, *stop and ask again*. In the beginning, you'll get two or three strides of good canter, then four or five, then half the perimeter of the arena, etc. This seems to be slow, but as a matter of fact, will give you much faster results than the other method, that of the "pushing-pulling" way, by which you try to re-balance your horse as you canter.

How can you know that your horse has lost his balance? First, because you feel uncomfortable. But, to be more precise, the balance can be considered as perfect only when you can drop the reins without destabilizing your horse; at a canter, for instance, without the horse speeding up noticeably.

At a trot or walk, the balance is imperfect if you cannot at any given time, engage the horse in side stepping with all his body ("leg yielding" of the modern Dressage, or "real shoulder-in" of La Guérinière).

How to Establish the Balance?

1) Contraction is the main enemy to balance, so try first to *avoid contractions* by the quality of your riding: "liquid" seat, soft hand, passive

legs as long as there is no need for transition; moderated aids for transitions.

2) Avoid untimely demands. For instance, if you ask for a canter right lead as your horse has his right front foot on the ground, you risk upsetting him, for he cannot respond to your demand as long as his right front foot is bearing all his weight.

Untimely demands are a main source of imbalance. This book will give you the precise timing for each of your actions, for each movement.

3) Practice flexions of the lower jaw (see Part Three; Sections X & XI).

To sum up, the principle of optimization of orders states that:

1) A demand from the rider should not be made before the horse has been set in the required balance;

2) The demand should not endanger the balance by its untimely character;

3) One must stop and relax the horse at the first manifestation of imbalance in the execution of a movement.

The author, Paris, 1963.

The author, trotting backwards, 1980.

PART TWO

Schooling of the Aids

I. The Seat

Three aspects have to be considered: the position, the weight, the seat.

Position

The position of the rider is most important because the torso, acting as a "balancing rod" (Nuno Oliveira), is a powerful aid, whose influence increases as the horse's collection perfects itself.

For this aid to be implemented, the torso should be constantly kept more or less *back from the vertical*, because it provides the rider with more *power* and more *balance*.

More power: As you are sitting on your horse, ask a person on foot to come and face him, and grab the snaffle reins, one in each hand. Then, ask this person to pull backwards with all his/her weight on the reins. The only way for you to resist this traction and prevent your friend from falling will be to use your torso as a buttress by sitting back.

The matter is not to start a tug of war with your horse, the matter is to outweigh, *if necessary*, your horse's neck so that you can, at any time, prevent him from falling on his shoulders. After that you will, of course, practice the release of aids.

More balance: As you sit on your horse, and even if you are very supple and almost disjointed at the hip level, your legs cannot be completely vertical; they point more or less forward. Hence, their center of gravity lies ahead of your buttock bones. If, in the meantime, your torso is leaning forward (hunt seat) or vertical (modern Dressage), the general center of gravity of your body will be ahead of the base of support which the buttock

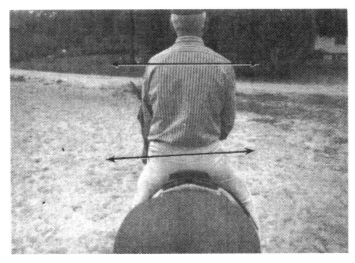

Fig. 1 - Pelvis tipped to left but shoulders keep a horiozontal line.

Fig. 2a - Pelvis tipped over.

Fig. 2b - Pelvis tipped under.

Rider's torso keeps same incline.

bones are (or should be). Try, in this position, to *completely* open your legs, avoiding even any contact between your thighs and the saddle, and you will immediately feel the need for sitting back.

Conclusion: The position of balance is with your torso *back from the vertical.* Hence, your weight will apply vertically over your buttock bones, your legs will be able to relax and give their cues with a maximum of efficiency.

The knees of the rider should, of course, be placed as low and far back as possible in order to achieve the maximum extension of the thighs, *but this should never be achieved at the expense of the correct position of the torso.* If, for lack of suppleness, your choice is between sitting back and having your knees a bit too high, or the other way around, opt for the first formula.

Weight

The rider's weight comes first as a nuisance for the horse because, besides the additional load it creates, it also wobbles.

But as soon as the rider has learned how to control this wobbling, that is, to maintain his torso parallel to itself in any circumstance, the weight can become a very determining aid.

Since the rider should strive to keep his torso imperturbably stable no matter what, the shifts of weight should be done by a mere displacement of the pelvis. The weight is brought to the right when the pelvis tips to right; to the left when it tips to left; forward when it tips over forward (arched back); backward if it tips under backwards (rounded back).

The lateral tippings of the pelvis should not alter in the least the horizontal setting of the line of shoulders, and its fore and aft rotations should not change the general incline of the torso. *This is most important (Fig. 1 & 2a, 2b).*

Only when the horse is fully schooled will unobtrusive "balancing rod" movements of the torso be introduced. Although invisible to the onlooker, these movements will display a surprising efficiency, due to the exquisite degree of balance attained by the horse.

How the weight aid works, however, is sometimes confusing, because a same cue can bring about two opposite results, depending on the situation.

Usually people think that a horse will alter his movement in the direction of the weight displacement. This is true only if the center of gravity of the ensemble "horse+rider" is being brought outside the vertical of the base of support. Over a jump, for instance, if the rider leans to the right the horse won't have any other alternative than to place his feet as much to the right as he can as he lands. On the finish line of a flat race, a jockey can stretch his horse by coming a bit more in front. Locomotion, in a way, is nothing else but a controlled fall; all the more so in a race. The horse's reaction, to control the fall, while he benefits from the momentum, is to bring his base of support forward under the center of gravity. Hence, the stretching.

But this is double edged, for if the horse feels that he cannot afford the supplement of speed required by this alteration of balance, he will tend to slow in order to fight the imbalance by lessening the momentum.

Therefore, the horse can feel the weight displacement as an incentive or as a burden. In the first case, he will endorse it by altering the movement in the direction of the cue; in the other case, he will oppose it, by moving his body in the other direction.

This latter case is by far the most common.

If, for instance, at a halt, walk, or slow trot, one loads a given lateral, the horse will tend to push from this lateral in the direction of the other, in order to even up the load respectively borne by each of these laterals (see Part Three, Section IV, **Shoulder-In**).

Therefore, if the rider's pelvis bears rightwards, the horse will tend to bear to the left and vice-versa. If the pelvis bears backwards (rounded back), the horse will tend to push from rear to front by disengaging his hind legs and flattening his back. And, if the rider's pelvis bears forwards, the rider arching his back, the horse will tend to slow and engage his rear end, thus rounding his back and collecting his frame.

So much so that the ensemble, "horse+rider," can appear as two spines perpendicular to each other which interact antagonistically: when the rider's spine rounds itself, the horse's hollows and vice-versa.

This probably explains why, in all the highly-collected horsemanships (baroque period, bull fighting), the riders display such an arched attitude.

Whichever explanation one gives to this phenomenon, the fact remains that *arching the back* stimulates a spontaneous reaction of collection even with an insensitive horse. For example, try to do this: at a walk, completely open your legs so as to suppress any contact from the crotch down, arch your back as you keep your shoulders in a back position, and try to "push" (at least in mind) only with your buttock bones, which are, at this moment, your only point of contact with your mount. Nine times out of ten you will observe a neat reaction of collection with the horse, although (or perhaps, because) your legs are not on.

For this, it is preferable not to ride in one of those stiff Dressage saddles, which usually dim the relation between the rider's seat and the horse's back.

The Seat, as Such

The seat is more than an aid: it is the aid of the aids. On its quality depends the good implementation of the two other aids.

RELAXATION is the master word.

Apart from the fact of sitting back as you keep your navel forward, don't foster any strict position prerequisites whose only effect would be to make you stiff. Especially, don't try to give any particular place to your feet: let them be where gravity places them. If they are too far forward, it means that you are contracted, and the same if they are too far back.

Three citations from French riders:

1) "Let yourself be seated" (Aubert, 1836).

2) "Then in the 23rd Dragoons, Colonel Faverot had an admirable position of legs. It made him easily recognized from afar and, in the dorms, the troopers were evoking it constantly: the legs, always immobile, were hanging vertically as are the stirrup leathers with an unmounted horse" (Beaudant, 1943).

3) "The good position on horseback is that of an experienced rider who has taken two valiums" (J.-C. Racinet, 1990).

Two excerpts from the Rule Book of the French Cavalry (1912):

1) "If the knees are correctly turned inwards, the muscles of the thigh find their place under the femur, and the thigh lies naturally on its flat part. The position of the knee entails that of the foot, which hangs normally..."

2) "It remains understood that the correctness of the position must come second to the necessity of the *pliability on horseback*..."

How to Adjust your Stirrups

Drop the stirrups and let your leg hang normally. Don't try to give it any particular position. Then raise your toe and try to put the stirrup on. If you are obliged to raise your knee, your stirrup is too short. If you are not obliged to raise your toe, your stirrup is too long (*Fig. 3*).

[13]

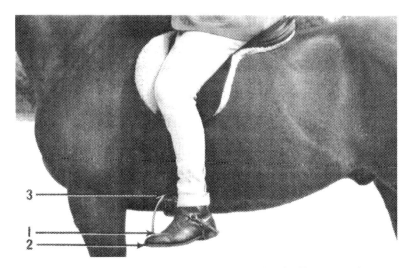

Fig. 3 - Adjustment of stirrups. 1 - Correct length.   2 - Too long: the rider would be "fishing" for his stirrups. 3 - Too short: the rider would have to rais knees in order to put stirrups on.

Fig. 4 - The rider's pelvis should be more forward, his back somewhat dished, his neck and shoulders should relax.

Fig. 5 - Same exercise with shorter stirrups;
same shortcomings with the rider.

Fig. 6

Exercises

Exercises to perform from the lunge line: (the horse should not have any reins, or the reins should be twisted under the horse's head and kept together by the throatlatch; the rider is not allowed to touch the reins *nor grab the pommel*).

1) Halt. Raise and stand upon your stirrups, as vertically as possible; that is, bring your pelvis way over the pommel (*Fig. 4*). Your thighs must be vertical. Lower the heels. Keep the position. Don't use your arms as balancing rods. Don't move them. Don't contract your shoulders. Don't collapse in front of the saddle. Don't back up your feet excessively.

Keep the same position at a walk, at a trot, and at a canter.

Don't try to keep your balance by all means; when you feel that you are losing your balance, just relax and sit back. When you sit back, bend the knee; don't move your foot forward.

Don't gesticulate with your hands; don't grab the mane. Any help, even the slightest, allows your back not to do its job. You are allowed to take a support on the neck, if you fall forward.

The purpose of this exercise is to supple and strengthen together the muscles commanding the play of your lumbar vertebrae, and to force you to arch your back in order to accompany the horse's movement.

Although practiced with stirrups and out of the saddle, this exercise has a direct influence on your riding without stirrups and seated in the saddle (sitting trot), for it nurtures exactly the required muscles.

This exercise is also excellent for jumping.

2) Same exercise, varying the length of the stirrups (*Fig. 5*).

3) Posting trot. No reins, but hands as if you had them. Rise and stand up. Post. Rise and stand up. Post...

The transition from standing up trot to posting trot should be crisp and easy. This teaches you how to relax all at once the muscles of your back.

4) Knees up, above and in front of the saddle, the lower legs in front of the flaps. Walk and trot. Don't grab the pommel; don't use your arms or hands as balancing tools (*Fig.6*).

This exercise teaches you how to set your torso correctly. It makes you ride "with your torso" and become aware of its importance in riding.

5) At a walk and trot, knees up, above and in front of the saddle, lower legs in front of flaps. Open the thighs (as much as you can). Hold this position for one second, then lower and relax your legs *very, very slowly and without changing the angle of your upper body (Fig. 7, 8 & 9)*. The

[16]

Fig. 7

Fig. 8

Fig. 9

Fig. 10 - Rider's right knee should be higher. Right hand should hang loosely, so as not to be in the way of the right leg's movement.

Fig. 11

Fig. 12 - The rider's left foot should toe still more inwards.

Fig. 13

Fig. 14

*Fig. 15 - The purpose of this exercise, which is only partly fulfilled here, is to forward the inside hip of the rider. The rider's right foot should toe **down** and **in**, the leg being stretched open. The outside leg should keep it normal position.*

interest of the exercise lies in this slow descending of the legs, as you stick to your horse only by the skin of your buttocks.

6) Sitting trot (no stirrups, no grabbing on the pommel). Rhythmic and alternate elevation of the knees: "one, two, three LEFT -- one, two, three RIGHT -- etc." Try to kick your shoulder with your knee (Fig. 10). If you can't help grabbing the pommel in the beginning, do it with the right hand as you lift the left knee, and vice-versa. Keep the other arm out of the way.

7) Sitting trot (no stirrups, no grabbing of the pommel). Rotation of one arm (Fig. 11). Rotation must be slow, arm must be stretched, rotation must be made in a vertical plane, the hand rising in the part of the circle which is in front of the rider. Follow your hand's movement with your eyes.

8) Torsion of the spine by a brisk rotation of the line of shoulders, outwards, then inward. When the line of your shoulders reaches a direction parallel to that of the horse, the knee of the side opposite to the rotation must try to "punch" the flap (Fig. 12).

9) Walk, trot, and canter. Pat your horse on the croup, as far back a possible, right side of the croup with your left hand and vice-versa (*Fig 13*).

10) Walk and trot. Without raising the knee or bending over, grab your right foot at the instep with your right hand; pull up briskly (in order to somewhat "force") and drop immediately. Same to the left (*Fig. 14*).

11) Canter (no stirrups, no reins, no hold on pommel). Stretch completely the inside leg, toe inside and down. Don't lift the knee (*Fig. 15*).

12) Halt. Inside knee stretched open, inside foot parallel to the horse, slide laterally in the saddle by tipping your pelvis as if you were falling outwards. Keep your inside thigh on the saddle by its inner part (hence, the requirement for the foot to remain parallel to the horse). Quit sliding as you feel you're about to fall. Come back into the saddle by a brisk movement *of your pelvis* (no help from the hands, no pommel, no "balancing rod") (*Figs. 16a through 16c*). Same exercise with the other thigh. Same at a walk and, if you have guts, at a trot.

A variation of this exercise consists of kicking downwards with the leg in order to help the coming back into the saddle. Less profitable for the strengthening of the rider's back, but very efficient.

Fig. 16a

Fig. 16b   *Fig. 16c*

Fig. 16d

[23]

This exercise is meant to teach riders how to come back in the saddle upon losing their lateral balance, by a mere movement of their body and avoiding hooking on the reins.

One could not stress too much the necessity for the students, even by their first lesson, *NOT TO GRAB THE POMMEL*. Better stay at a halt than to walk while holding the pommel...at a walk than trotting with the help of the pommel, etc. The rider must learn how to stay on horseback thanks to his body's balance, and not through a traction on the reins.

The instructors who, under the pretexts of progressiveness, kindness, psychology, etc., allow beginners to take the pommel by their first lunge lesson are doing these beginners a disservice.

II. The Hands

Adjustment of Reins

1) To *start* the adjustment of the reins:

At a halt: Take the reins by their extremity in the right hand alone, raise this hand enough to give the reins some tension, extend the other hand and take the two reins *between your thumb and index finger*.

Fig. 17

Extend your right hand in turn, divide the reins up, holding them at first between thumb and index. Keeping the tip of your thumbs on the reins, extend the other fingers in a medium position, making the hand ajar, so that it can work two ways, either by opening or by shutting (*Figs. 17, 18, and 19*).

This gives you a first adjustment, which will probably have to be

Fig. 18

Fig. 19

completed in order to attain the *exact* length of reins allowing the best and easiest riding possible.

2) To *complete* the adjustment of reins:

a) Lengthening: Let the reins *slide* between your fingers, the tip of the thumb remaining on the surface of the rein, the "plier" thumb-index maintaining a slight friction. Block the reins at the desired length by clenching the "plier" thumb-index (*Fig. 20a*).

b) Shortening: Take both reins in the right hand by bringing the left rein under your right thumb, extend the left hand ahead of the right hand, grab both reins with the left hand (using only the "plier" thumb-index, or the three first fingers of the left hand, the index being, in this case, inserted between the reins - attention to keep your thumb on the reins *by its tip*, free your right hand, bring it next to the left, divide the reins up (*Fig. 20b* and c).

Then, as the horse goes, constantly modifying its frame, you will have to *maintain* the adjustment of the reins.

3) To maintain the adjustment of the reins, you should keep your elbows free from contraction so they can constantly bend and unbend. If

Fig. 20a - Lengthening the reins.
Thumbs are shown open in order to give a stronger impression of
"release." They should, however, be gently shut, checking by their
tip the eventual sliding of the reins.

Fig. 20b

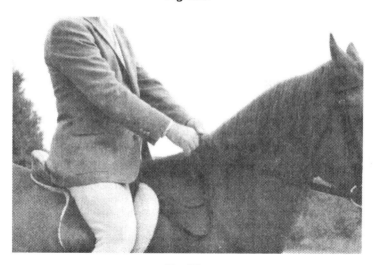

Fig. 20c

you have to bend (or, worse, tip over) your wrists in order to keep a constant contact with the horse's mouth or for whatever reason, it is the infallible sign that your elbows are blocked.

95% of the riders have their elbows blocked.

The freedom of the elbows, their ability to bend and unbend in order to follow the horse's mouth, is an absolute prerequisite to any good horsemanship.

In the beginning, have somebody check on you. Old reflexes are hard to kill.

Exercise

At a walk, trot, canter, very progressively shorten your reins up to the utmost possible, then lengthen them very progressively, keeping the same speed with the horse. Especially, the speed should not decrease as you shorten the reins, or increase as you lengthen them.

Repeat this exercise often, until a permanent and subtle readjustment of the reins has become a reflex with your riding.

Closing and Opening the Fingers

1) *Closing:* Press the thumb by its tip on the rein without tipping over your wrist, maintaining this "plier" thumb-index at an even distance from the body (through a momentary blocking of the elbow and shoulder). Squeeze the other fingers progressively, *from top to bottom.* This action entails a slight rotation of the wrist, by which the hand comes into a more vertical position.

Fig. 21a

In this action, the fingers have to be brought toward the palm, and not the other way around, which would produce no effect (very common shortcoming).

2) *Opening:* Extend all the fingers to their maximum length. This movement makes the palm face down.

3) Fingers can act, resist, or give.

They *act* when they clench on the reins (make a fist).

They *resist* when they remain in an "ajar" position.

They *give* when they open completely, *with the exception of the "plier" thumb-index.*

Stopping and Slowing Down

Exercise

At a halt, unbuckle the reins, pass them behind your back, and tie them up again behind your back by means of a knot. Adjust the knot so there is tension on the reins when your torso is vertical (*Figs. 21a and 21b*).

Bend over enough to liberate the horse's mouth. Use your legs and walk. Keeping your legs carefully off the horse, sit up and, in so doing, stop your horse. The halt should be immediate and easy. If you are

Fig. 21b

[29]

obliged to lean back in order to get the desired result, your reins are too long. Tighten up the knot. In all this exercise, keep your hands off the reins.

VERY IMPORTANT REMARK: The author has practiced this exercise with hundreds of his students without any trouble whatsoever. This comes from the fact that the action of the rider's torso is so efficient that the horse yields to it with no defense.

Still, it is preferable to perform it indoors or, if one has any misgivings, on a proven calm horse.

The instructor may also, as he/she prefers, keep the two reins joined in his/her right hand behind the student's back, as he/she proceeds with the exercise.

This exercise is meant to show you the tremendous power of the back in stopping a horse, once the reins have been adjusted. Subsequently, you will try to retrieve the same feeling as you stop with the reins in hand.

A careful adjustment of the reins is an absolute prerequisite. Adjusting the reins (as you ride the standard way) amounts to tightening the knot correctly behind your back in the previous exercise. The adjustment of the reins may require a recoil of the hands by bending the elbows (i.e., your hands are allowed in this case to come nearer your body, but only in this case; as they *act*, the hands should *never come closer to your body*).

As a rule:

1) If the purpose is to establish a good contact with the horse's mouth, or give the reins the proper direction of action, your hands are allowed - nay, required - to move;

2) If the purpose is to *act*, the hand must remain immobile. The action is provided either by the fingers (clenching), or by the torso (reclining), or by both.

A very common error, for the student who starts using this "torso stopping technique," consists in yielding with the arms as the back reclines, which negates the action of the torso. So keep your hands at a steady distance from the body during the duration of the proceeding, if necessary, by blocking your elbows and shoulders.

This blocking is very short, since the action should not exceed one-half second (remember, "Moderation of Aids").

Another very common shortcoming is to lower the hands as one tries to stop. Don't. As an exercise, and to compensate, try to lift your hands as you stop. You probably won't succeed in really elevating them much, but at least it will help you in keeping your hands steady.

Stopping vs. Slowing

There is no difference of intensity (strength) between the actions of stopping and slowing, but a mere difference in *duration*. A slowing down is nothing else than an uncompleted halt. If you can slow, you can stop (you just have to go on slowing down to a halt), so if you can stop, you can slow (you just have to shorten the duration of your stopping action).

If we call the action of the torso by which we have stopped a horse going a slow walk a "unit of stopping," slowing down a horse from a high speed will require several of these "units," and coming to a complete halt will require still more of them.

But, in any case, the action has been "pulsated."

Turnings

See Part Three, Section IV, **Bending a Horse**.

Specific Actions on the Lower Jaw

See Part Three, Section VIII, **Flexion of Jaw**.

III. The Legs

Leg of Impulsion, Leg of Position

For the forward movement, place your heel next to the girth (leg of impulsion). To move the croup sideways around the shoulders (single leg), position your heel back from the girth.

IMPORTANT REMARK: Upon proper conditioning (see further), the leg's action is *always* impulsive. The lateralizing effect of the single leg stems from an appropriate opposition of the hands (see Part Three, Section VI).

Action of the Leg

Use the lowest possible part of your lower leg -- that part situated just above the place of the spur. *Don't press with calves.*

IMPORTANT REMARK: The rider must learn how to "round" his leg along the horse's side in order to reach as low as possible, possibly under the belly (depending on the proportions between horse and rider), where the skin is sensitive.

Press enough for the horse to feel that something is going on; keep this pressure one hundred percent even, steady, as long as you have not reached the speed you want to get. Although you don't increase the pressure of the leg (heel), be insistent, don't wobble, make up for the undulations of the horse's body as he proceeds forward.

As soon as the horse has reached the desired speed, release totally and instantly the action of legs. If then the horse slows, *let him slow quite neatly*, then apply a second action in order to restore the speed and release again, etc. In time, the horse will understand that *he* has to maintain the speed as it has been brought about by your leg action.

Pay attention not to increase the frequency of your actions of legs — you would end up pushing constantly (i.e., associating a steady action of leg to a steady movement). Given the "associative" aspect of the horse's mind, this association would be fatal to your leg's power, since the horse would equate your leg to a mere *maintenance* signal and not a signal for *transformation* (acceleration). So *space up* your leg actions accordingly.

The horse must answer your leg action by moving forward if at a halt, or accelerating if in motion.

If the horse's answer to your leg is uncertain or sluggish, give him the lesson of the leg.

Lesson of the Leg

From a halt, apply a standard pressure of legs (heels). If, after one second, the horse has not moved forward, *DON'T PRESS MORE, DON'T PRESS LESS — ADD THE CROP*. Upon the horse's jumping (hopefully) forward, open the legs and pat profusely.

Generally, two or three of these actions suffice to make the horse understand the meaning of the leg action. If then, you observe carefully the principles of release, separation, and moderation of aids, the horse will become sharper and sharper to your legs.

As a rule, in any circumstance when the horse ignores your leg order, *don't press more, don't press less — add the crop*. But bear in mind that this sudden ignorance, from the horse, of the rider's legs, probably results from errors in your riding, mainly a non-observance of the two first principles (release and separation of aids), which has progressively *untrained the horse* (i.e., undone his conditioning to the action of legs).

The goal is to equip the horse with a reflex of unconditional forward movement when the legs show up, and unconditional acceleration as long as their presence lasts. The brain is no longer concerned, the reflex centers take the procedure in charge, and even though the horse is distracted or "lazy," his response will be guaranteed.

The center of all this schooling is the careful avoidance of any simultaneousness between any steady action of leg and any steady speed. This simultaneousness can happen only in two cases:

1) Either the horse has reached the desired speed, and the rider has not released his/her action, or;

2) The horse has quit accelerating even though the rider's leg is still on, since the desired speed has not been attained, and the crop, which should have been used immediately, has not been applied.

PART THREE

The Conquest of Collection

I. Lightness and Collection

Lightness

Lightness is the absence of resistances of weight or strength to the actions of the hands, and the absence of resistances of inertia to the actions of the legs.

There is resistance of *strength* when the horse "pulls" on the rider's hand.

There is resistance of *weight* when the horse "bears" on the rider's hand.

There is resistance of *inertia* when the horse "ignores" the actions of legs.

It is evident that once these resistances disappear, the horse answers the slightest indications of the aids. He then becomes framed between the "weight of the reins and the stroke of the boots."

It is to be noticed that the more a horse becomes light to the hand, the more he becomes light to the legs, since he benefits from a better balance. And, to a lesser extent, but neatly enough to be acknowledged, the more he becomes light to the legs, the less he is likely to display contractions in his front end.

To some extent, lightness depends on the rider as well as on the horse, for the best of horses, if ill ridden, will momentarily lose its lightness. And on the other hand, an experienced rider will sometimes make light a horse who had been, until then, considered heavy.

Lightness is obtained by observing the principles of release, separation and moderation of aids, and by the practice of relaxation of the lower jaw (see Section VIII).

[35]

Fig. 22

Collection

First experiment: Measure your horse (at the withers), as he is grazing. Then measure him again as his head is in a normal, average position. Then lift his head and neck as much as you can, from the ground, and measure him another time. You are going to get three different measurements, and find out that your horse's size increases with the elevation of his head *(Fig. 22)*.

Second experiment: Your horse being saddled, but unmounted, measure him (if possible on a very hard ground; a cement slab, for instance). Then have somebody mount the horse, and take a new measurement. You'll find out that your horse's size diminishes when mounted.

These two experiments illustrate the fact that a horse has no collar bone (clavicle) and that his withers and first ribs are kind of "floating" between his two shoulder blades; the liaison, at this level, between the spine and the rest of the skeleton being only assured by muscles and

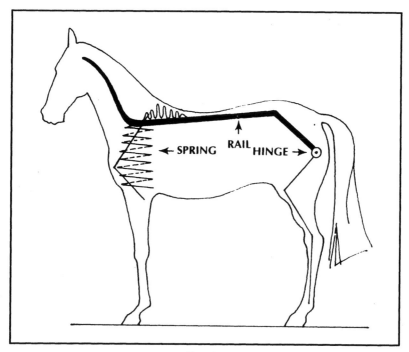

Fig. 23

ligaments. It is a supple - and somewhat weak - liaison, whereas in the other direction, toward the rear, there is a bone to bone connection.

So much so that the spine of the horse could be schematically represented by a strong horizontal rail, angled at one extremity (the haunches) and hinging around an axis (the coxa-femoral joint), whereas by the other extremity, it lies upon a big, cylindrical spring. Beyond that area of support, the rail takes the shape of an ascending "S" (neck and head) *(Fig. 23)*.

If a load is brought upon the rail, part of it will be borne by the cylindrical spring, which will be compressed, and whose vertical dimension will diminish more or less, depending on its strength. The strain brought upon the spring will be all the more important as the load comes nearer the spring. For instance, if the load is situated at mid-distance between the spring and the hinge, only half of it will bear on the spring. If the respective distances between the load and the spring on the one hand, the hinge on the other hand, are in the rapport of one to two, the

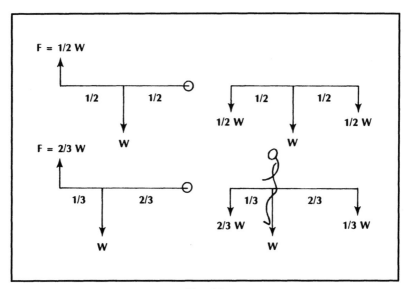

Fig. 24

spring will bear two-thirds of the load (that is, the reverse proportion, according to the theory of levers) *(Fig. 24)*.

Harmful Effect of the Rider's Weight

The effect of the rider's weight is threefold:
1) It crushes the withers area, bringing about contractions which impair the horse's ability to balance himself.
2) It overloads the front legs of the horse in a proportion of two-thirds of the rider's weight, against only one-third on the rear legs (according to experiments made by Baucher in the 1850's; yet, the simple reasoning would probably have led to the same conclusion, given the average place of a rider's seat on a horse's back).
Bearing in mind that the usual division of the horse's own weight is of five for the front against four for the rear (according to the previously cited experiments by Baucher), the horse's natural balance is slightly altered toward more load for the front, because two-thirds is bigger than five-ninths.
3) And, finally, the horse has to deal with a total weight now superior to his own, that is, a weight increased in a proportion of about 10%;

he is in the situation of a 150-pound athlete who has to run with an overload of 15 pounds.

To counter these three harmful effects of the rider's weight, the horse will:

1) Try to raise his withers. For this he will use the muscles of this very area, but more than likely, he will also tip under his haunches, whose power will be necessary to hold up the whole spine. This will amount to shortening the "medium line" of the horse, which links the edge of the shoulders to the edge of the buttocks.

2) Engage, more or less, his hind legs under his body, in order to make them take more weight and, in so doing, restore the natural division of the masses to its ordinary value of five for the front, against four for the rear.

3) Display more energy in the action of his hind joints, mainly hocks.

Now it happens that these three very features: shortening of the medium line (edge of shoulder - edge of buttocks) by elevating the withers and tipping under the pelvic area, additional engagement of the rear legs under the body, and increased activity of the hocks are the three main features of collection. It hence stands out that collection is nothing else than the attitude which allows the horse to *negate the impairment brought about by his being ridden, and retrieve the balance he displays when free in a pasture.*

Of those three features, the most important one is the shortening of the medium line, by which a horse upholds his withers and keeps his croup in a more or less "tipped under" attitude (forwarding of the edge of buttocks). This feature really defines collection. When it is absent, so is collection *(Fig. 25)*.

Collection and Engagement

Collection should not be mistaken for the engagement of the hind feet under the horse's body. At a counted walk (see Section Two) or at a piaffe, there is little engagement of the hind hooves under the body, though the horse is collected. In a free walk, where the horse is allowed to extend his frame and slump his withers, there may be a great engagement of the forward-moving hind leg, though the horse is all sprawled out.

At a halt, or at a canter (where the two hind legs engage and disengage practically together), the engagement of the hind feet may, or may not, bring about the forwarding of the edge of buttock, hence the tipping under

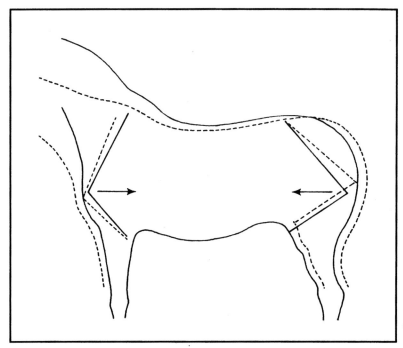

Fig. 25 - Contraction of the medium line.

of the pelvic bone.

At a walk or trot, the engagement of one hind leg is the result of the disengagement of the other hind leg. These two actions contradict each other as concerns their possible influence on the tipping under of the pelvic bone. So when a horse engages considerably one hind leg, he disengages the other, and this does not mean, in the least, that he has tipped under his pelvic bone. It just means that he is making big steps or strides.

One should remember that the engagement of one hind leg under the body proceeds almost entirely from the shutting of the coxa-femoral joint and the opening of the stifle, both of which are fairly bendable and extendable. Horses have little limitation in this realm, as we can observe when, for instance, a horse scratches one of his ears with a hind hoof.

Indeed, by forwarding the edge of buttock, the tipping under of the pelvic bone may add to these possibilities of engagement, but there is really not much need for it.

So much so that the *engagement of hindquarters*, which the tipping

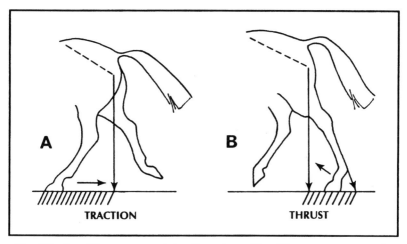

Fig. 26 - A = Disengagement, traction phase. B = Disengagement, push-ing phase; the horse backs its rear leg by flattening its croup.

under of the pelvic bone is, and the *engagement of the rear feet* appear as two distinct phenomena.

Still, although bearing little significance as concerns the engagement of the hind feet, the *engagement of hindquarters* will alter definitely the gaits, through the *limiting effect* it has on the *disengagement of the hind legs.*

This calls for a little analysis.

The old cliché has it that a horse engages his hind legs under him in order to better "push" forward. This should be called into question. The gesture of engagement, in itself, has no motor value because, as this gesture develops itself, the foot has no contact with the ground. As a matter of fact, it is the gesture of *disengagement* which is motor.

This latter gesture presents two phases.

In the first phase, the horse *pulls himself* on the ground, his hind joints remaining bent, and displaying no other effort than keeping the leg stiff enough to operate the *traction*. This first phase ends when the foot reaches the vertical projection of the edge of buttock. In this phase, if the croup keeps an unchanged angle, which is the case when a horse is collected, the movement results only from the opening of the coxa-femoral joint.

Then comes the second phase, where the horse really *pushes*, since the foot has passed behind him. This phase is much more efficient, because it benefits from the unbending of the hock. With the uncollected horse, this phase profits also from a backward flattening of the croup, which gives the hind hoof more liberty to reach back *(Fig. 26)*.

Collection comes as a handicap for this second phase, because it limits the possibilities of disengagement of the foot by preventing the croup from flattening backwards, keeping the edge of the buttocks in an unchanged forward position *(Fig. 27)*.

Consequently, the spring action of the hocks will have to work more vertically; the gaits will get more elevated.

The motion will also have to rely more on the first phase of the disengagement movement. The horse will have to learn how to *pull his mass more energetically* on the ground, which is a somewhat unexpected conclusion with respect to the conventional equestrian wisdom.

Collection and Fixity of the Head

When a horse is not collected, at a walk or at a canter, he moves his head to and fro. This is explained by the fact that, during each stride or step he makes in these gaits, he also rotates his pelvic bone to and fro, in order to give more strength to its rear thrust, which takes all its meaning once the hind legs pass *behind* the horse's body.

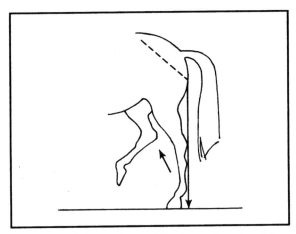

Fig. 27 - Collected horse. Tipping under his pelvis prevents rear foot from backing up. Thrust applies more vertically.

This movement of the head and the accompanying flattening of the croup imply a rhythmic alternation of bracing and loosening of the muscles of the back.

At a trot, however, probably due to the fast rhythm with which the strides follow each other, this alternation of muscular tension and release in the horse's back is made, if not impossible, at least very difficult, and this probably explains why the phenomenon is not seen in this gait. The back's tension remains even, which means that the croup keeps an unchanged angle, and the head remains more or less immobile.

This, of course, does not mean that the trot is by essence a collected gait, for it is not only the *fixity* of the croup which defines collection, but its important degree of forward rotation.

In other words, if at a walk or canter the fixity of the head expresses at least a beginning of collection, it does not have the same meaning at a trot.

Collection and "Ramener"

"Ramener" is a French equestrian term which designates a head set where the forehead is vertical, as the poll remains the highest point of the neck curve.

This magnificent attitude *always* accompanies the perfect collection but, unfortunately, does little to create it. Its premature systematic and separate enforcement, as an absolute prerequisite to any work, may bring about severe disappointments. The Arabian horses, or American Saddle-breds presented in Equitation shows, often display a perfect ramener, although their backs are awfully flat, if not hollow, and their hindquarters disengaged.

On the other hand, Dressage horses prematurely "Ramené'd" by a backward action of the hands usually bear on the bit, have a tendency to overflex their neck and often display stiff, brusque, down transitions. They sure are "on the bit," but too much, and to what avail?

The conquest of "ramener" takes as much time as that of collection, whose most exquisite expression it constitutes. This does not mean that separate flexions of the jaw, neck, and shoulders should not be applied in the process of the training, but they do not suffice; they just help, and the horse has to be worked also in his ensemble.

Many riders are literally stuck in a rut, because after having set the head in what they deem to be a correct position, their horse's balance is on the shoulders, and they can only move forward at a steady speed. Any up or down transition, any attempt to lateral work, would destroy this so dearly acquired "prettiness" of the front end.

One must bear in mind that gracefully arching a horse's neck has never set him on the haunches, whereas a horse set on the haunches, regardless of the prior position of his head is much more likely to come gently onto his bit, provided that the rider gives subsequently the hand and leaves the horse in "liberty on parole" through a "descente de main" ("release of hands"). Complementary actions of the fingers may then be waged in order to perfect the "ramener" so obtained.

Collection and Lightness

There cannot be lightness without collection, because an uncollected horse does not have the necessary balance to answer the orders of his rider immediately when the matter is to practice tight evolutions. There hence will be resistances, at least of inertia, and more than likely of strength, also.

Yet the collection has to be *self-maintained from the horse*, if one wants lightness to evidence, so that the rider's aids can be disengaged. If the rider's aids cannot be disengaged, it means that the horse is *bearing* on them, which negates the notion of lightness. This proves two things:

1) First, that if lightness entails collection, collection does not mandatorily entail lightness (Vienna).

2) Second that the systematic, obstinate seeking of lightness in all the stages of riding *leads mandatorily to a permanent and self-maintained collection*.

Collection and Extension

To speed up, a horse must increase — together or separately — the length of his strides or steps and the tempo of the gait.

Rapidly, however, the horse will have to make a choice between increasing the length of the stride or step and revving up his tempo, because he has attained the maximum physical work he is able to produce. Depending on their temperament, some will opt for long and slower strides, whereas some will precipitate the rhythm at the expense of the length of the strides.

In Academic riding, the goal of extending the gaits is not to attain a very high speed; it is to "magnify" the horse's gaits by showing them in the plenitude of their development. We can be assured that this goal will be reached if we can urge the horse to accelerate, *as we require him to maintain the slowest possible tempo.*

These two requirements, of course, are more or less antagonistic, and it will take some time before the horse understands that he is required to speed up, but *only by means of extension of the gesture,* since he is not allowed to accelerate his rhythm.

The only way to maintain a slow tempo is to keep the horse seated on his haunches; in other words, collected. This collection entails, let it be reminded, the tipping under of the pelvic bone and the consequent lifting up of the withers. In an extension, as soon as the withers "collapse" because the back cannot brace up any longer, the gait precipitates and the extension of the gesture diminishes more or less.

In other words, extension is not the opposite to collection. On the contrary; it is the *expression of collection in speed.*

Let it be acknowledged here that collection is not a constraint inflicted upon a gait in order to give this gait a momentary brilliance at a slow speed; it is a constraint inflicted upon the structure of a horse in order to give his gaits a permanent brilliance at all the stages of their development. And the fact that collection is easier at a slow speed and with a schooled horse does not mean that we should limit its practice to old horses at slow gaits.

This goal of permanent collection, whatever the speed, can only be attained if the horse displays *self-collection.* Self-collection is obtained through a systematic release of the aids, during all the process of the training.

For lack of enforcing the principle of *release of aids,* modern Dressage sets itself in the obligation to *limit the notion of collection to slow gaits.* Hence, the sequence "collected trot, working trot, medium trot, and extended trot," as if collection were absent from working, medium, and extended trots.

For the FEI system of Dressage, extension *negates* collection.

For Riding in Lightness ("Horsemanship of French Tradition"), extension *expresses* collection.

II. Counted Walk

Take an inside line (keep away from the wall of the arena). Walk as slowly as possible, taking the chance of a halt. Slow the walk with your back only (ref. Part Two, Section II, **Stopping and Slowing**). No legs; legs only to start or restart. If the horse stops, try first to *open the fingers* before using the legs; perhaps the horse will start again without the help of the legs.

Keep very straight. If the horse "wiggles," "counter-wiggle," using one rein at a time (if the horse's croup comes to left, resist with the left hand, right hand if the croup comes to right). When using one rein, slightly open the fingers of the other hand.

The horse must be light. If the slowness is maintained through a strong tension of the reins, the exercise is void of interest. If the horse bears on the bit, give the hand, then take again.

Let the horse raise his head and neck as he wants. Don't try, in the beginning, to position his head in a low and tucked position; that would make the exercise almost impossible.

When the horse understands that he cannot accelerate, cannot stop, cannot offset his haunches, he takes the movement in charge (self-impulsion and self-carriage). Then he raises spectacularly his withers, walking as if he were "tip toeing." The steps are neatly separate from one another; the walk proceeds from an instant of quasi-immobility to another instant of quasi-immobility, linked by a kind of sliding step with the front legs...a little like in the parade march of the British Grenadiers.

The beat of the hind legs becomes suddenly stronger. Whereas, in a normal walk, one hears more the beat of the front feet, in this case, the beat of the hind feet becomes prevalent. The rider feels with great neatness the beat of one hind leg, accompanied by the sudden bending in the joints of the other hind leg, as if that leg were "breaking," allowing the precipitate grounding of the other hind leg. The advance so taken by the hind leg which comes to the ground tends to give the walk a diagonal character, which is one of the main interests of this gait (see Part Four, Section I, **Mechanism of the Gaits**).

In addition to all this, the horse will display unobtrusive and spontaneous flexions with his lower jaw (see Section VIII, **Flexion of Jaw**).

Spectacular elevation of the withers, diagonalization of the gait, marked beat of the hind legs, and spontaneous flexions of jaw are the four features that characterize a good counted walk. The term counted walk is explained probably by the fact that the rider can almost withhold each step and let it drop at will, as if he were dropping drops from an eye dropper.

[46]

What should be slowed, in a counted walk, is not so much the speed as such, as the tempo. Once requested to go in a counted walk, some good horses extend spontaneously the gesture of their front legs; they then perform a school walk, one of the most beautiful gaits a horse can display.

As a rule, the more one slows a walk, the more this walk tends to diagonalize (see Part Four, Section I, **Mechanism of the Gaits**). However, the rule bears exceptions. When slowed down, some horses tend first to diagonalize their walk, but then, beyond a certain degree of slowing, they lose this diagonalization and alter the gait. With these horses the slowing down should not exceed this threshold, lest one deny to counted walk all its educational value.

The counted walk is the best possible education for collection, since it provokes a drastic shortening of the medium line, entailing together a maximum elevation of the withers and a complete tipping under of the pelvic bone.

The exquisite balance created by this exercise may be taken advantage of for teaching difficult movements such as side steps ("leg yielding"), shoulder-in, half-passes (see Sections V & VI).

Improvement of the "Ramener" through Counted Walk

After a few steps of a perfect counted walk where the horse is self-impulsed, light and self-cadenced, open slightly the fingers and let the horse come just a bit more on the shoulders and extend his frame, *but without losing the elevation of the withers*. The horse will then lower his neck and come spontaneously on the bit. Complete the "ramener" through alternate and delicate actions of the fingers, "kneading" the reins.

The advantage of the ramener so obtained is that it occurs upon a *release* of the hands, and not a traction.

From this collected walk, try a slow trot, *without losing ramener and lightness*. If one of these two factors deteriorates, or both, come back to a counted walk and do the operation all over again.

III. Up and Down Transitions

Accelerate and Slow Down Within the Gait

Accelerate: The horse having been trained to the leg action as explained in Part Two, Section III, content yourself with applying a steady leg action until the desired speed is attained. Keep your fingers open as you use your legs (ref. Part One, Section II; **Hand Without Legs, Legs Without Hand**). The horse must maintain the speed; he should not slow down, neither should he go on accelerating once the impulsive order is off.

Remember: Acceleration while keeping the tempo at its slowest brings about extension of the gait. The legs should bring about the extension, but not accompany it (ref. Part One, Section III; **Release of the Aids**).

Extensions should be asked for very progressively — they must remain a joy for the horse.

Decelerate: Pulsated actions only, operated more by the back than by the hand itself (ref. Part Two, Section II). Don't lower the hands during the whole process. You may clench your fingers occasionally to give the action more firmness. The distance between your hands and your body should remain constant.

When properly done, the slowing actions remain practically invisible. Don't wiggle in the saddle.

Upward and Downward Transitions

The gaits are a horse's gear box: walk is the first gear, trot the second gear, and canter the third. Like with an automobile, gears have to change when a certain speed is attained. Energy saving is the principle underlying all this. A horse will trot when he feels that accelerating the walk would require much pain for little result, and the same for trot to canter.

So the simplest way to pass from one gait to another is to accelerate or slow down - there will almost mandatorily come a moment when the horse decides to change his gait.

But this way is very primitive, for we are entirely depending on the horse's decision; he may or may not slide into the next gear exactly when we want it to happen.

Therefore, to the slowing or accelerating actions of the hands or the legs, other cues should be added which will tend to *transform* one gait into another, regardless of the speed. These cues have an action on the *mechanism* of the gaits and will allow the rider to make a new gait appear, or sustain the same gait, at speeds somewhat different from those which, otherwise, would have justified them.

Halt to walk: Both legs, symmetrical. Open the fingers as you come with your legs. If you want to start by a given front leg, indirect rein on the side you want to move first (for the definition of indirect rein, see Section IV, **Bending a Horse**).

Halt to trot: The most difficult of all. Very discrete half-halt on both hands, then open the fingers and come with the legs. The action of legs does not need to be "energetic." But it must be very "insisting," though very even. The difficulty is to avoid the departure into a canter. Horse must be very straight.

Halt to canter: Very easy. No hands at all. As an exercise, you may try to abandon the reins completely and grab them back as you canter. This exercise is not dangerous; the horse is less likely to bolt away than if you had the reins.

The secret lies in the steadiness and firmness of the action of the *inside heel* near the girth. Push this heel onto the horse's side toward the girth, as if you were kicking a soccer ball with it. Don't forget, in the meantime, to press your outside heel back from the girth. Avoid sliding your outside leg in a pendulum movement which doesn't bring any result (very common shortcoming). Although back from the girth, the outside heel must apply a perpendicular pressure onto the horse's side.

Walk to trot: Left leg (at the girth) when the left hind foot hits the ground (or right leg when the right hind foot hits the ground).

This is explained by the fact that immediately after a hind foot has come to the ground, the horse will be on a diagonal base, for the duration of a half step (see Part Four, Section I; **Mechanism of the Gaits**). Since the trot is a diagonal gait, it is easier for the horse to start a trot when he already is on a diagonal base.

Trot to canter: Young horse — medium trot on a circle. Crop in the outside hand. Each time the outside front foot hits the ground, tap the outside shoulder with the crop. This action must be well adjusted to the horse's gait and light enough not to entail acceleration. After a few taps the horse will take the canter on the inside lead, practically without accelerating from the trot.

When the horse understands well and responds by the very first tap, associate the action of outside leg to the crop, then finally use only the outside leg.

Schooled horse — outside leg (back from girth) when the outside front foot hits the ground. This transition should not provoke any acceleration.

The advantage of this way is that the cuing is totally different from that meant to extend the trot. Hence, there cannot be any confusion in the horse's mind, which is extremely profitable as far as extensions are concerned.

Canter from a walk: Outside leg during all the time the outside front foot is on the ground (i.e., when the rider sees the outside front limb moving back). Departure is very crisp; the horse poses his inside front leg and then starts with the outside hind leg very engaged (first beat of the canter; see Part Four, Section I; **Mechanism of the Gaits**), so the canter is "seated."

This exercise is an educational tool for flying changes.

Canter from an accelerated free walk: The walk must be *very energetic.* Outside leg when the outside shoulder is swinging forward. No hands at all.

The canter so obtained is usually very light, horizontal, perfectly on three beats and active in the haunches, although slow in tempo. Excellent for flying changes.

Canter from a rein back: Ask with the outside leg when the outside front foot hits the ground. At this very moment, the outside rear (first beat of the canter) is fully engaged, so the horse will "jump" forward, projecting his outside diagonal *and* his inside fore, which he has to hold up, because it has to hit the ground after the outside diagonal. So during a short time, the horse pushes with his outside rear, while the three other feet are in the air. This, indeed, gives a lot of expression to the departure into canter.

Trot from canter: Somewhat difficult. Slow the canter but, although you slow, try to lengthen your reins in order to let the horse "fall" on his front end. *Keep your horse very straight* and use your hands alternately, in rhythm with the grounding of the front feet, but *in a crossing manner* (i.e., that the left hand is used when the right front lands, and vice-versa).

A simplified version consists in fixing the inside hand (horse straight) and using only the outside hand rhythmically, when the inside front foot lands (third beat of canter).

All this works all the better as one takes care not to elevate the horse's head (long reins) which would collect the horse and tend to keep the horse cantering.

Walk from trot: This is the most important, most educational of all. Adjust the reins carefully and then close the fingers of the right hand when the horse's right front foot hits the ground, and close the fingers of the left hand when the left front foot hits the ground.

Don't "pull" with your arms; use only the fingers and apply the action on the reins, as if you were kneading some paste in your palms. Don't move the hands. As a matter of fact, if your reins are correctly adjusted, and if you position your hands as taught in this book (i.e., with your fingers ajar *but for* the "pincers" thumb-index, your elbows remaining supple so as to maintain a faithful contact with the horse's mouth), you won't have to close your fingers much and still will get an outstanding result.

Remember: Bring your fingers toward your palm, not your palm toward your fingers.

This procedure will bring about supple, progressive and harmonious transitions, producing an energetic walk. The back of your horse will literally "swing" and relax.

By "breaking up" the trot, this action of direct accompanying with the hands of the grounding of the front feet forces the walk to appear at a speed slightly superior to this which would have otherwise justified this gait. Hence the energy of the walk so obtained.

But attention — the horse will ask to extend his frame in order to sustain this energetic walk. Give the hand accordingly.

Upon this extension of the horse's frame, it may be very opportune to ask for a trot again. The horse will then answer the slightest indication of your legs. Ask for a walk again (by this method), and upon the horse extending his frame at a walk, immediately ask for a trot, etc.

This will work your horse's back wonderfully.

Slowing the canter beneath the speed limit of trot: Slowing action of the hands must operate *by the end of third beat*, and during all the suspension time. It ends with the first beat of canter, as the horse starts a new stride.

Slowing of trot beneath the speed limit of medium walk: Cross-accompany with the hands (right hand when left front foot lands and vice versa). Use the legs *only to* prevent the horse from walking, if necessary.

IV. Bending a Horse

For instance, bending to right...

1) Bring head to right, if necessary through an "opening rein" (the right forearm rotates to the right; no or very little movement with the arm *(Fig. 28)*.

In the meantime, let the left rein slide between the fingers of the left hand (ref. Part Two, Section II; **The Hands - Adjustment of the**

Reins, 2a). Do not move your left hand forward; your two hands should remain in the same position as if you were riding a straight horse *(Fig. 29)*. Simply, your left rein is longer than the right. If the horse yields thoroughly, there is not more tension in the right rein than in the left.

2) Bring your right hand back toward the center line of the horse (withers). *Most important* (see **Remarks & Justifications**; para. 2 *"Experiment"* for the explanation; *Fig. 30)*.

3) Offset your weight to right (ref. Part Two, Section I; **The Seat - Weight**; *(Fig. 31a, b, c and d)*.

4) If necessary (most times, it won't be), complete the bending action with right heel. As the horse yields, quit using this heel (ref. Part One, Section III; **Release of Aids**). *Do not maintain the bending through a constant application of the inner leg; you would set out for heaviness.*

Remarks & Justifications

1) When you offset your pelvis to right, your right hand moves to right by the same token. So you should *compensate* by an additional movement of your right hand *to left*, so as to maintain this right hand in its very place.

2) *Experiment:* After having brought your horse's head to the right, first keep the right rein in the direction of the *right hip* of the horse, and then ask somebody on the ground to come to the left side of the horse and push with the hand on the left hip of the horse, so as to move the rear end to the right.

You will observe that, try as he or she may, this person *cannot* push the horse's croup to right because your right hand, resisting in the direction of the right hip of the horse, *blocks completely this possibility* *(Fig. 32 A)*.

Then bring your right hand to the left, toward the withers, in the position of the "indirect" rein, and resume the experiment. You will then observe that the more you try to resist the person's thrust in this position, the easier it is for him or her to push the horse's croup to right *(Fig. 32 B)*.

This explains why, after having brought the head to the inside by a direct (schooled horse) or opening (young horse) rein, your hand must take the position of the indirect rein, which does not prevent the croup from moving inward.

3) When one puts weight upon a leg of a horse, the right fore, for instance, the horse is not inclined to move this leg. On the contrary,

Fig. 28

Fig. 29 - Outside hand incorrect.

Fig. 30

Fig. 31a

[53]

he will take support from this leg and move his mass toward another leg (the left fore, most probably) in order to re-establish what his balance was prior to this overload.

If one loads the whole right lateral, the horse will try to move his mass from this lateral, toward the left one. But, since you keep his head to the right, he can do this only by bending his spine, back from his shoulders, to the left.

Therefore, this combination of hand resistance and displacement of the weight is most likely to help transmit to the whole of the horse the bending which is first exhibited in the front end.

Changing Rein

To pass from bending to right into bending to left:

1) Set your left rein under your right thumb. Both reins, right and left, are now between your right thumb and index *(Fig. 33)*.

2) Reach out with your left hand ahead of your right hand, take the left rein between thumb and index first, the other fingers ajar *(Fig. 34)*,

Fig. 31b - Horse bent to the right. Rider's seat slightly offset to the right. Left elbow symmetrical to the right elbow.

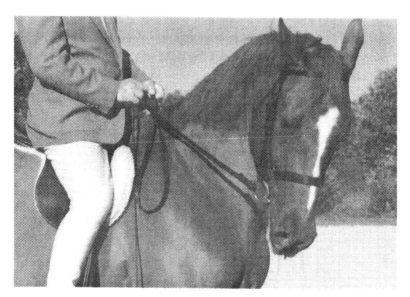

Fig. 31c - Horse bent to the right, horse and rider seen from the right.

Fig. 31d - Horse bent to the right, seen from the left. Left rein longer than the right rein, but some tension. Both hands on the same line.

bring your left hand back near the right in its standard position *(Fig. 35)* and, in the meantime, *let the right rein slide between the fingers of the right hand* and then block the right rein with your right thumb *(Fig. 36)*.

3) Offset your weight to left to complete the horse's new bending *(Fig. 37)*.

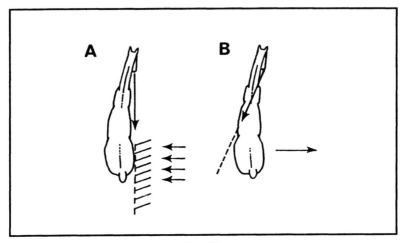

Fig. 32

Fig. 33

Remarks:

1) Allowing the outside (outside-to-be) rein to slide between the fingers until it has reached the convenient length, in order not to oppose the shortening of the inside (inside-to-be) rein, should become absolute *REFLEX.*

2) In no case should the outside (outside-to-be) hand move forward in this operation. The outside arm must remain near the torso so as not to alter the balance of this part of the rider's body. Most often, as the outside hand is brought forward, the trunk is tipped inward; the rider is no longer correctly seated.

3) Let it be recalled here that the rider's weight is offset laterally *through a mere tipping of his pelvis,* the trunk remaining upright and its weight remaining *evenly divided* over the two buttock bones.

Circles

If a horse, upon being bent, is set into motion, he traces a circle, *provided that* the bending and the speed remain even. The aids are not engaged constantly; they are momentarily wielded to *restore* occasionally the speed and bending, if they vary, in order to maintain the regularity of the circle.

Leaning on a Shoulder (inside or outside)

In both cases, this evasion results from an insufficient bending of the spine between shoulders and croup. The spine, more or less straight, then pushes diagonally toward one shoulder or the other, depending on the position of the croup. If the croup was set inward when the spine stiffened, the thrust will be applied onto the outside shoulder. If the croup was more or less out of the circle, the thrust will apply toward the inside shoulder.

1) *Leaning outward:* Soften the action of the inside hand, take and give, or rather give, and then take again, etc. Most often this suffices to bring the horse back on his circle. Apply several soft, intermittent actions rather than only a plain one.

If this is not enough, add a pulsated action of neck rein on the convex side (outer side) of the neck. Since the action of the inside rein is also pulsated, these two actions of reins must be *alternate,* the neck rein acting when the inside rein yields, and vice-versa.

2) *Leaning inward:* With the inside hand, pull the horse still more inside

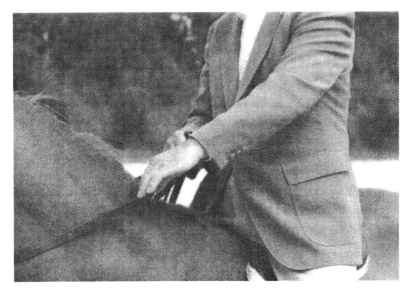

Fig. 34

Fig. 35

Fig. 36

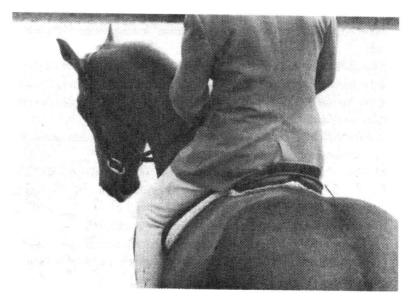

Fig. 37

than he wants to go and, in the meantime, push with the legs. In a reaction to your demand the horse will try to escape sideways with his shoulders; therefore, he will come back to his circle.

Never attempt to chase the shoulders out if the neck itself is already more or less bearing outward. *First bring the head way inside, AND THEN ONLY apply an indirect rein,* which amounts, in fact, to executing the procedure described in the above paragraph.

Effects of Reins

The following terminology is singular to the author of this book. It has been established for instructional reasons. However, the actions hereunder described encompass the standard effects of reins of the French traditional riding, as they appear in other books.

1) *Sliding Rein:* The most important of all, though nobody ever speaks of it. It consists of opening the fingers, the hand remaining immobile, and allowing the rein to slide until it reaches the convenient length. Then, close the fingers, mostly the thumb over the index, the other fingers remaining "ajar" in a medium position.

The action of "sliding rein" is always wielded on the outside rein, which plays a most determining part of "fulcrum" for the action of the inside rein.

The daily experience shows that this role of "fulcrum" is better fulfilled if the hand remains in its place, near the torso (which can only be done if the fingers are first "permissive"), than if the hand moves forward with no release of its grip on the rein.

2) *Elbow Rein:* Block the elbow and resist in the direction of the hip on the same side.

Blocking the elbow means that you maintain its bending; *DO NOT LOWER THE HAND.* If the hand had to move backwards, this would have to be done *in the direction of the elbow.*

Elbow rein may be wielded on the inside or outside rein.

3) *"Tummy Rein:"* Inside rein (mostly, but sometimes outside, as well). Forearm rotates toward the rider's stomach, then the hand fixes itself and resists. Arm does not move, or very little.

This rein is the opposite of the opening rein.

Inside "tummy rein" is commonly (and somewhat improperly) called "indirect rein," because *if (and IF only) the outside rein offers the proper resistance,* it may move the horse outward more or less laterally.

4) Opening Rein: Executed through an outward rotation of the forearm only, the elbow immobile and kept near the torso, as a mere "pivot" (ref. **Bending a Horse**, para. 1).

Remarks:

1) All three effects of the inside rein (opening, elbow, and "tummy") *must always be accompanied by an outside sliding rein.*

2) Their effect depends then entirely on the modulating action of the outside rein (resistance through an "elbow rein"). If there is no resistance at all, "tummy rein" as well as inside elbow rein entail curvature for the horse (with better yielding as concerns the "tummy rein").

The graduated resistance of the outside rein brings about:

a) Inside "tummy rein:" Shoulder-in, counter shoulder-in, turning around the haunches (see Section V).

b) Inside "elbow rein:" Side steps (or "leg yielding," but here the lateral effect is 100% obtained from the hands; the legs are only impulsive and applied only if necessary), shoulder-in on a circle, turning around shoulders (see Section V).

V. Shoulder-In

Shoulder-in is a lateral movement in which a horse is bent opposite to his direction of march. If a horse, bent to right, moves laterally to left, he performs a right shoulder-in. If he is bent to left as he goes to right, he is in a left shoulder-in *(Fig. 38)*.

Generalities on Lateral Movements

In a lateral movement a horse does not go straight forward, he proceeds sideways, "crab like."

Two quantities only suffice to define most precisely any lateral movement: the *angle* of movement, and the *curvature* of the horse.

The angle of movement is the angle formed on one side by the direction of movement and on the other side by the general direction of the horse.

The direction of movement is easy to grasp, since most often it is rectilinear (straight). If ever the movement were describing a curve, the direction of movement at a given point would be defined by the straight

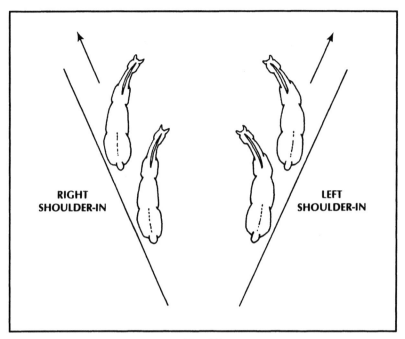

Fig. 38

line tangent to this curve at this given point *(Fig. 39)*.

The direction of the horse is more difficult to define as the horse may display some bending. If one considers that the horse's spine is drawing an arc, the direction of the horse is determined by the chord subtending this arc. Practically speaking, it is the segment of straight line that links the middle point of the line of shoulders, to the middle point of the line of haunches *(Fig. 40)*.

The curvature of the horse is easy to define by the radius of the circle the horse's spine is drawing an arc of *(Fig. 41)*.

The angle of any lateral movement cannot exceed ninety degrees, lest we see the horse "back up laterally" *(Fig. 42)*.

Since shoulder-in is basically an exercise, it may be performed on any given angle; the rider chooses the angle which fits his or her purpose of the moment. However, the angles usually practiced range between 30 and 45 degrees.

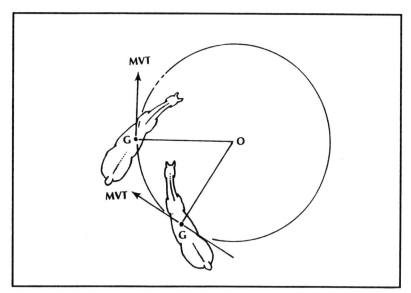

Fig. 39

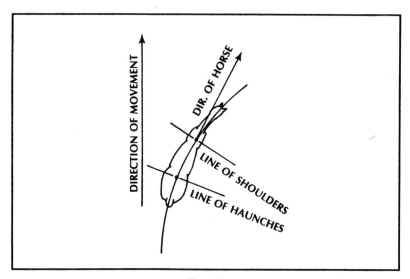

Fig. 40

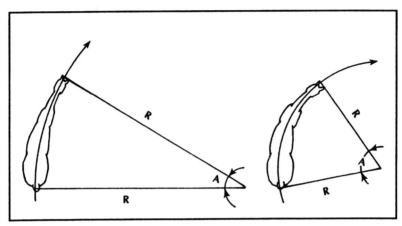

Fig. 41 - As the lateral bending of a horse augments, the radius R diminishes and the angle A increases.

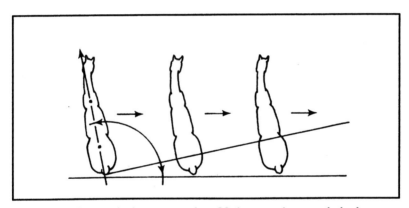

Fig. 42 - The angle A is greater than 90 degrees. As a result the horse backs up laterally.

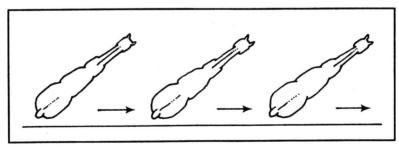

Fig. 43 - Lateral movement with no lateral bending with the horse.

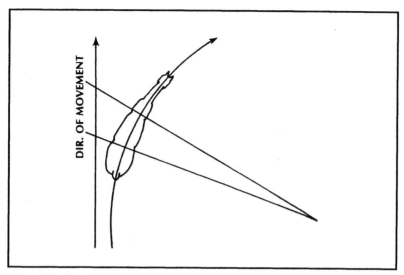

Fig. 44 - Shoulder-in. Since the horse is bent, the haunches are less aslant. with respect to the movement than the shoulders are.

Relation Between Angle of Movement
and Curvature of the Horse

In a lateral movement, if a horse is not bent, the line of shoulders and the line of haunches remain parallel to each other, thus they display the same obliquity with respect to the direction of movement *(Fig. 43)*.

In a shoulder-in, as the horse is bent, the line of shoulders and the line of haunches do not remain any longer parallel to each other; they diverge, and do not display the same obliquity with respect to the direction of movement. And, since the horse is bent opposite to his direction of march, the shoulders show more obliquity than the haunches *(Fig. 44)*.

So it is easy to understand that, by a certain degree of bending for a given angle of movement, the haunches will cease to be aslant with respect to the direction of march. At this level, the movement will cease to be lateral *(Fig. 45)*.

If the angle of movement is important, this will require quite a strong degree of curvature and, since a horse has only limited bending possibilities, this is not likely to happen *(Fig. 46)*.

But as the angle of movement lessens, this possibility gets stronger.

[65]

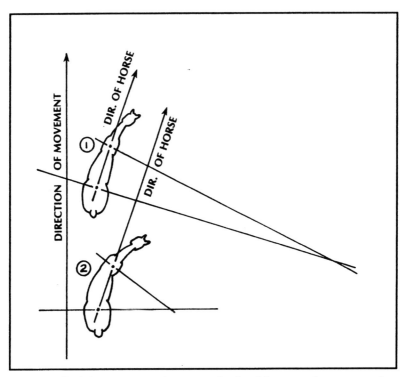

Fig. 45 - Both horses are performing right shoulder-in on the same angle, but here horse 2 is overly bent, which brings his haunches to the direction of movement.

The rider should be aware of it and proportion the degree of curvature of his horse to the angle of movement, *so as to prevent this from happening.*

The obliquity of the haunches with respect to the movement (i.e., the fact that the hind feet are positioned, on the ground, in a slanted manner with respect to their track line), is *indeed an essential element* in a shoulder-in, which gives it all its value *(Fig. 47).*

The horse's hind joints, in effect, aren't built to bend laterally. Therefore a horse, in order to engage his inside hind leg in a slanted manner, is obliged to *tip off his pelvis* in the meantime, as he sets himself more on the haunches, by bending the joints of his outside hind leg.

If the haunches were going square, this advantage would be lost, and the movement deprived of its meaning.

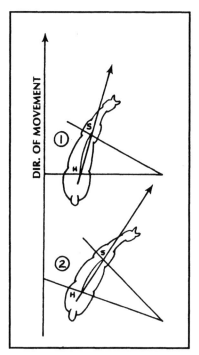

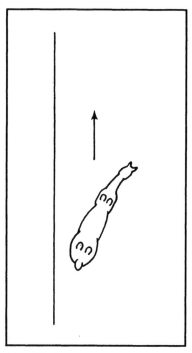

Fig. 46 - Horse 1 represents horse 2 in Fig. 45. Same angle of shoulder-in, same bending, same result: haunches are square to the movement. Horse 2 is horse 1 of preceding figure. Same bending, but bigger angle in the shoulder-in. The haunches come aslant anew with respect to the move-

Fig. 47 - In a shoulder-in the hind feet, like the front feet, set down aslant with respect to the movement.

The fact that the hind feet, as well as the front feet (but somewhat less, due to the fact that the horse is bent), set down on the ground aslant with respect to the direction of movement expresses the lateral character of this movement (Figs. 48 and 49).

This entails, practically, that the inside legs of the horse cross over the outside ones. This crossing over is more or less important, depending on the energy of the action, and the degree of laterality, and is always more evident in front than behind, as a result of the bending. As a matter of

Fig. 48 - Right shoulder-in at trot; crossing of the front legs.

Fig. 49 - Right shoulder-in at trot; crossing the hind legs. The crossing is less important behind than in front, due to the lateral bending. In fact, the right hind foot sets down in the front, that is, in the alignment of the outside rear. Both rear feet set down slantwise with respect to the direction of movement.

fact, most often the crossing gesture of the hind legs is only started; the inside hind foot setting down *in front of* (i.e., in the alignment of) the outside one (*Fig. 50*).

History of Shoulder-In

Shoulder-in was introduced first by French rider François Robichon de La Guérinière, equerry of King Louis XV, in his book *Ecole de Cavalerie* (1731), whose chapter XI is entirely devoted to the subject.

The diagram (page 197 of the edition of 1769), as well as the whole text, shows that:
- the angle of movement is about 30 degrees;
- four tracks are traced on the ground;
- the hind legs set down aslant with respect to their track line;
- the inside legs, rear and front as well, cross over the outside ones, although very little;
- the bending of the horse is very moderate.

The goals of shoulder-in, for La Guérinière, are:
- to supple the shoulders by teaching a horse how to freely cross his front legs one over the other;
- to lower the inside hip, by virtue of the crossing gesture of the inside hind leg over the outside; hence to prepare the horse for collection;
- to accustom the horse to move away from the inside heel in order to move freely laterally.

The aids of shoulder-in, for La Guérinière, are:
- inside hand, and;
- inside leg.

Notice that La Guérinière comes at a "slow and slightly restricted walk" (*Ecole de Cavalerie, p. 197*) along the wall. Then, he turns the horse's shoulders inside, as if he were starting a circle, and "...when he is in this oblique and circular posture, one should make him go ahead along the wall, with the help of the inside rein and leg; which he absolutely can't do, in this attitude, without crossing the inside front leg over the outside, as well as the inside hind leg over the outside..."

"Shoulder-in" is a somewhat insufficient translation for the French "épaule en dedans:" "shoulder inside" would have been more appropriate, since the purpose of La Guérinière, under the circumstances, was to stress the fact that the shoulders must be placed inside of the arena, on an inside track, before the movement was started.

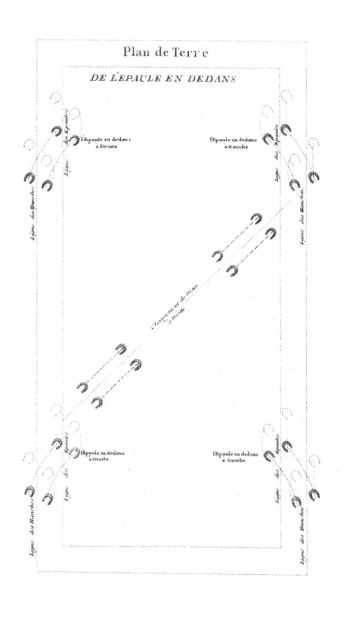

Diagram of shoulder-in as seen by its founder.
(La Guérinière, 1731)

"Shoulders-in" (as proposed by the Portuguese Master Nuno Oliveira) would also have been appropriate.

The Germans, as well, have mistranslated "shoulder-in," in a very revealing way. The German language, in effect, distinguishes "hinein," for a movement which goes away from the subject, from "herein," which applies to a movement coming to the subject. And, since the shoulders are placed on an inside track *away from their previous position*, the correct translation should have been "Schulter hinein," and not, as it happens, "Schulter herein."

Evolution and Alteration of Shoulder-In

There are two notions in shoulder-in — the lateral character of the movement and the fact that the horse is bent. Those two notions may be separated — on a circle, a horse is bent and does not go laterally; in a "leg yielding," or "side steps," the horse goes laterally and is not bent.

It is the conjunction of the two which makes the specificity of shoulder-in; the bending of the horse prepares him to better lower his inside hip, the lowering of which will, in turn, be accentuated by the lateral engagement of the inside hind leg. The bending also, if correctly wielded *and limited*, incites the horse's front end to move laterally, away from the inside leg which this very bending overloads.

On the other hand, it is the lateral nature of the movement *at the level of the rear end* which sets a horse on the haunches and, in turn, by pulling the withers back and up, facilitates the crossing gesture of the front legs.

Any attempt to privilege one of those two notions to the detriment of the other deprives shoulder-in of its meaning and virtue.

The most common deformation consists in emphasizing the bending, while overlooking the lateral character of the movement.

This alteration is probably very old. It appears as far back as 1790 in a book written by the Portuguese author Manoel Carlos de Andrade, *Light of the Liberal and Noble Art of Cavalry*, which the Portuguese consider equal, if not superior to La Guérinière's. In this book, two differences come about:

1) Shoulder-in is the continuation of the work on a circle. Now, although he does not ignore this work, La Guérinière does not deal specifically with it, and even calls it "a punishment" (op cit. p. 184)! This linkage of the work on a circle to shoulder-in reveals a particular concern for bending in this latter movement, which does not show at

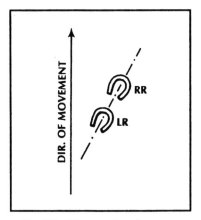

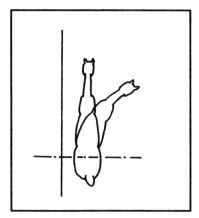

Fig. 50 - This is what the state-
ment "in shoulder-in, the inside
hind foot sets down in front of the
outside one" means: in the alignment of.

Fig. 51 - Shoulders brought inside
of the arena by mere bending the
horse (Steinbrecht). Haunches
stay square to wall.

all with La Guérinière.

2) The inside hind foot and the outside front have the same track. La
Guérinière does not elaborate on the number of tracks, but his diagram
shows four of them, with the outside front tracking neatly (albeit
moderately) beyond the inside hind.

This limitation of the angle of movement, added to the desire for a
more or less pronounced bending, involves the risk of the haunches
coming square to the movement, with the hind feet setting down in
the direction of march and no longer aslant with respect to it. *This, of
course, betrays completely La Guérinière's purpose.* In this matter,
Carlos Manoel de Andrade appears more as a precursor to Steinbrecht
than a disciple of La Guérinière.

The System of Steinbrecht (1808-1885)

Steinbrecht (*The Gymnasium of the Horse*, 1885), condemns any
lateral movement "without previous bending and collection" (as, for
instance, modern "leg yielding") as allegedly likely to ruin the horse's legs.
Therefore, he considers the lateral aspect of a shoulder-in as a conse-
quence of the bending of the horse and, he adds, "rather a secondary
phenomenon."

To place the shoulders on an inside track - unlike La Guérinière - he does not set the horse aslant *in his whole* (albeit with some eventual bending) with respect to the wall; he uses only the bending. And since a horse bends all the better as he is more schooled, he recommends to practice first with a slim obliquity.

Writes he, "The more a horse is bent, the farther apart the tract of his front feet will be from the tract of his hind feet, and the more the inside legs will have to cross over the outside."

This latter consideration, which is perfectly true as concerns the front feet, is by contrast totally erroneous as concerns the hind feet. In a shoulder-in, the more the horse is bent, the more the obliquity - hence the crossing-over gesture - diminishes with the rear end.

Steinbrecht doesn't seem to realize that, if the spacing of the front tracks away from the rear tracks results merely from the curvature of the horse's spine, *the haunches have no reasons in the least to alter their perpendicularity with respect to the wall*, and that there will be no lateral engagement at all of the inside hind foot.

But, at another point in his text, he states that the outside leg of the rider should carefully check the lateral movement of the outside hind leg of the horse, since this conditions the proper crossing of the inside hind leg over the outside.

The least we can say is that Steinbrecht, in this matter, lacks in clarity.

The FEI's Shoulder-In

This lack in clarity is further reflected in the FEI Rule Book, which states that a shoulder-in should be performed with a 30-degree angle but, due to the unworded (though very enforceable) three-track requirement, comes up with a drawing where the angle of movement measures only 13.5 degrees (*Fig. 52*)!

Also, the text states that the inside hind foot should set down "in front of" (instead of "in the alignment of") the outside hind, which is perfectly vague from a directional point of view. To top it off, on the diagram of the 1987 edition, the traces of the horse's feet are represented by small circles, which introduces one more element of uncertainty as concerns their position vs. the direction of march (*Fig. 52*).

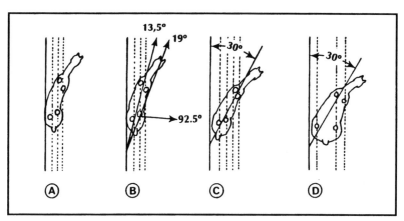

Fig. 52

A = Excerpt from the FEI "Rules for Dressage Events," p. 38. Reproduction of the drawing illustrating the shoulder-in (17th edition, 1987).

B = Same drawing with measurements of the angles. If the line joining the middle point of the shoulder line to the middle point of the haunches line is taken as reference for the direction of the horse's body, one finds out that the angle of the movement is only 13.5 degrees!

And if, to be more liberal, one takes the line joining the ears to the tail, one still finds only 19 degrees, which is far from the 30 degrees required by the text. The line of the haunches displays an angle of 92.5 degrees with respect to the wall, which means that the haunches are practically square to the direction of movement.

C = The same horse with same curvature, placed on a 30 degree angle with respect to the wall: four tracks are traced on the ground.

D = This drawing shows the proportions which a horse should have in order to display a 30 degree angle and, nevertheless, trace only three tracks on the ground!

How to Train Horse and Student to Shoulder-In

Shoulder-in is a difficult exercise. Some subjects — horses as well as students — are more gifted than others.
Exercises
Try the following exercises:
1) Bend a horse the way indicated in this book, and walk on a circle. When the horse is self-impulsed and relaxed on this circle, press with

the inside leg *near the girth* (very important), and in the meantime, resist a bit with the outside hand, either by a discrete "elbow rein," or by alternate pressures of the fingers. The horse will engage in a shoulder-in, away from the circle. Content yourself with one or two lateral steps and reward.

Remarks:

a) Do not modify the position of your seat and inside hand as you wield the inside leg and outside hand aids.

b) If movement lingers to start, slow the horse until result comes.

2) Counted walk. When the horse is light, bend him slightly. Offset your weight to the inside and, in so doing, try to induce a lateral movement *without any use of the inside leg*, if possible.

If you don't "feel," use the inside leg, but subsequently try to avoid using it.

More than anything else, in this exercise, it is the pressure of your inside buttock which determines the horse laterally.

3) Stop at the beginning of a middle line. Offset your seat on one side. Press *strongly* with the leg on the same side, near the girth, and walk forward. Let the horse go (i.e., give the reins).

What will happen is that, in spite of your having offset your seat and for all the strength of your inside leg action, the horse will go straight *because you give with the hands.*

Then, progressively but *without changing anything in your seat and inside leg action*, slow the horse for a counted walk. At a given point of this slowing process, the horse will, all of a sudden, *answer your seat and inside leg action* and proceed laterally.

Remarks:

a) In a shoulder-in, the hand *DOES NOT* determine a horse's lateral action. This role is imparted to the inside leg or the seat (better).

However, these latter aids alone have no effect; they need the assistance of the hand. This assistance comes about through a soft resistance, a "withholding" of the horse's front end. Any attempt to induce the lateral feature of the movement through a leading action of hands is doomed to failure.

b) It is often advisable to try to move very laterally first, almost in a "side pass," and as the horse gets accustomed to going laterally, to introduce progressively a forward component in the movement.

c) The bending may also be introduced progressively.

Shoulder-in at a Trot: To perform only when a horse is schooled to shoulder-in at a walk. More difficult. Check carefully the lateral component of the movement of the hind legs. Check also that the horse does not "walk" diagonally in his movement, but goes on "trotting" (i.e., bounces from one diagonal to the other).

Shoulder-in at a Canter: Right shoulder-in as the horse canters right lead; left shoulder-in for the left lead.

Very productive. Very difficult. Keep a slim angle.

Shoulder-in on a Circle:

1) Right shoulder-in on a circle to right (clockwise), or left shoulder-in on a circle to left (counter clockwise). The horse's head is within the circle. If you shorten progressively the radius of the circle, you end up turning around the shoulders (reversed pirouette in a counter bending).

This movement sets back on the shoulders a horse who is too much "seated" (very rare!) *(Fig. 53)*.

2) Right shoulder-in on a circle to left (counter clockwise) or left shoulder-in on a circle to right (clockwise). The horse has his croup within the circle. This - difficult - movement is named "counter shoulder-in."

If the circle shrinks progressively, the movement ends up in a turning around the haunches (pirouette in a counter bending) *(Fig. 53)*.

VI. Half-Pass

Half-pass is a lateral movement where the horse looks in the direction of march. It is a kind of "anti-shoulder-in" *(Fig. 54)*.

Half-pass is a very strenuous exercise because the direct bending is not favorable to a lateral movement. If, for instance, the horse is bent to right, he is more or less induced into moving laterally *leftward* (i.e., in the direction *opposite* to that we want him to go). This, of course, denies the principle of "optimization of orders" (ref. Part One, Section V), by which a horse has to be set first in the best possible conditions for the intended purpose, before he is activated.

This is one more reason to *scrupulously* try to abide by the other principles of riding in lightness, mainly that of release of aids. The rider will be very watchful to avoid a constant application of the aids during all the duration of the movement. The horse has to be left alone, as soon as he has been engaged in his half-pass, if only for one stride or step. Try

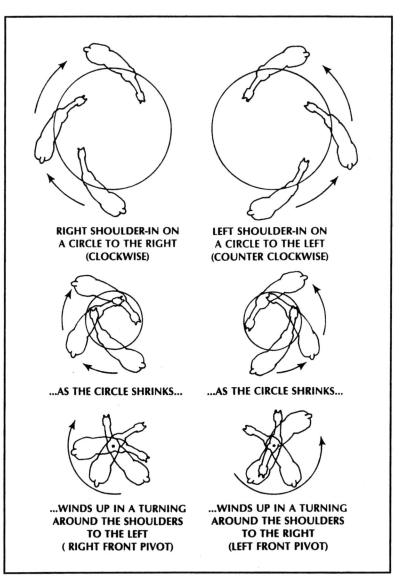

**RIGHT SHOULDER-IN ON
A CIRCLE TO THE RIGHT
(CLOCKWISE)**

**LEFT SHOULDER-IN ON
A CIRCLE TO THE LEFT
(COUNTER CLOCKWISE)**

...AS THE CIRCLE SHRINKS...

...AS THE CIRCLE SHRINKS...

**...WINDS UP IN A TURNING
AROUND THE SHOULDERS
TO THE LEFT
(RIGHT FRONT PIVOT)**

**...WINDS UP IN A TURNING
AROUND THE SHOULDERS
TO THE RIGHT
(LEFT FRONT PIVOT)**

Fig 53

progressively to get two, then three, etc. strides or steps of a self-main-tained movement.

The key to a good execution of a half-pass lies in the correct position

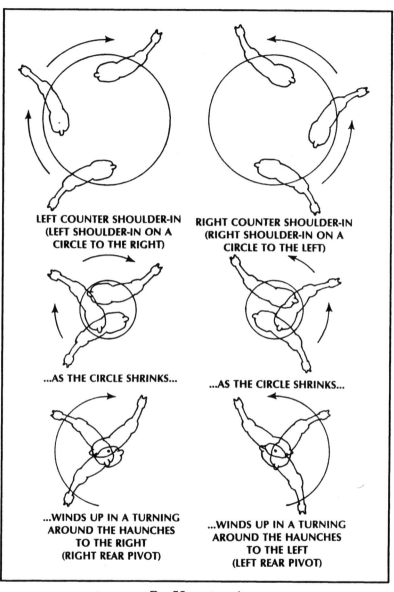

LEFT COUNTER SHOULDER-IN
(LEFT SHOULDER-IN ON A
CIRCLE TO THE RIGHT)

RIGHT COUNTER SHOULDER-IN
(RIGHT SHOULDER-IN ON A
CIRCLE TO THE LEFT)

...AS THE CIRCLE SHRINKS...

...AS THE CIRCLE SHRINKS...

...WINDS UP IN A TURNING
AROUND THE HAUNCHES
TO THE RIGHT
(RIGHT REAR PIVOT)

...WINDS UP IN A TURNING
AROUND THE HAUNCHES
TO THE LEFT
(LEFT REAR PIVOT)

Fig. 53 continued

of the inside hand, which must resist in the direction of the outside hip of the horse (ref. Part Three, Section IV; **Bending a Horse**). Keep the seat inside (in the direction of movement), mainly at a trot.

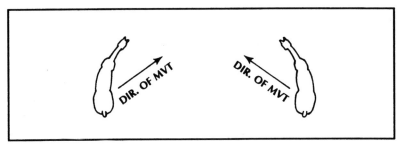

Half-pass to the right.   *Fig. 54*   *Half-pass to the left.*

Exercises:

1) Bend the horse. Walk on a circle. Bear laterally on a shoulder-in, away from the circle. Circle again (another circle, which is the like of the first), shoulder-in then circle, etc. *(Fig. 55).*

As you feel that the horse is perfect on his shoulder-in, come back onto a circle but *immediately* use the outside leg back from the girth, in

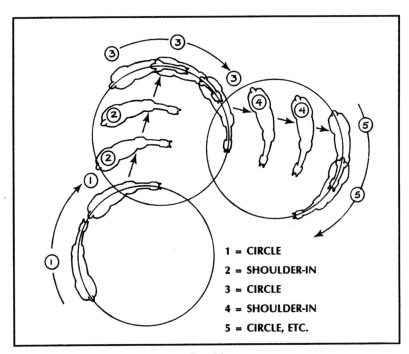

1 = CIRCLE
2 = SHOULDER-IN
3 = CIRCLE
4 = SHOULDER-IN
5 = CIRCLE, ETC.

Fig. 55

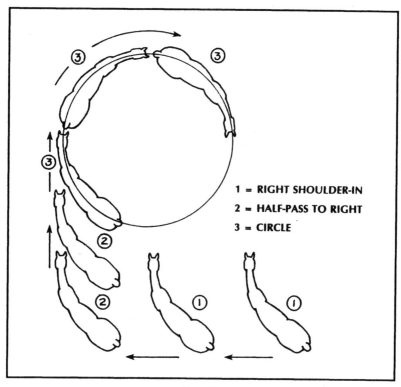

1 = RIGHT SHOULDER-IN
2 = HALF-PASS TO RIGHT
3 = CIRCLE

Fig. 56

order to chase the haunches *inward.* Tact is necessary with the hands. In the beginning, it may be useful to bring the seat back to a central position, nay slightly outward *(Fig. 56).*

Content yourself with one or two side-steps in this position, *and then push forward onto a circle with inside leg and hand predominant (Fig. 56).* Reward.

2) Counted walk. Slightly bend the horse to the right, for instance. Try to induce him to rightward lateral movement with soft action of the left leg back from the girth and, if necessary, soft, pulsated left neck rein. Very efficient.

Half-Pass at a Trot: To be started only when the horse is going easily in half-passes at a walk. Sitting trot, although it may be helpful, in the beginning, to post the trot *on the inside* (i.e., the "wrong") *diagonal* (because a horse's croup always tends to move in the direction of the

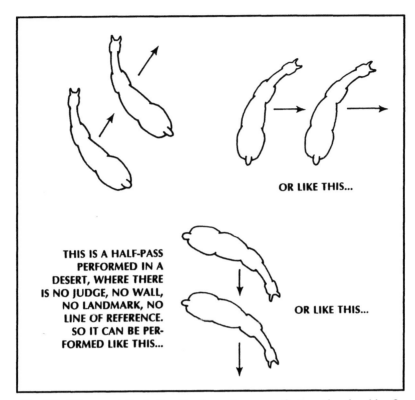

OR LIKE THIS...

THIS IS A HALF-PASS
PERFORMED IN A
DESERT, WHERE THERE
IS NO JUDGE, NO WALL,
NO LANDMARK, NO
LINE OF REFERENCE.
SO IT CAN BE PER-
FORMED LIKE THIS...

OR LIKE THIS...

Fig. 57 - Who can tell whether the haunches come first, or the shoulders? Yet it is a half-pass, no doubt about it. And in the three cases, the same movement:same curvature with the horse, same angle of movement.

diagonal on which the rider is trotting).

At the end of a half-pass, if there is enough room, send the horse forward and immediately turn him in the direction of his bending, in order to link, in his mind, the movement to the bending. If, at the end of a half-pass, the bending is systematically reversed, the horse will anticipate and lose his bending by the end of the movement; all the more since this bending is introducing an element of strain.

Half-Pass at a Canter: Slowest possible tempo. Sit back a little. Outside leg back from the girth, in rhythm with canter, *right after the third beat.*

In the beginning, to help the horse understand, it may be advisable to give up any requirement of direct bending, and even, *momentarily,* to

[82]

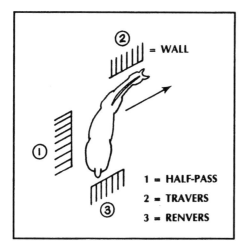

1 = HALF-PASS
2 = TRAVERS
3 = RENVERS

Fig.58 - Only the position of the wall has changed. The movement remains the same!

accept a counter bending (horse bent to left although cantering right lead, rightward).

If the horse resists by leaning, in his canter, onto his outside shoulder (second beat of canter), refusing to move this shoulder inward in the direction of movement, deceive him by *dropping the inside rein*. Very severe punishment. May be dangerous. Very efficient. After two or three attempts, the horse will forego his defense.

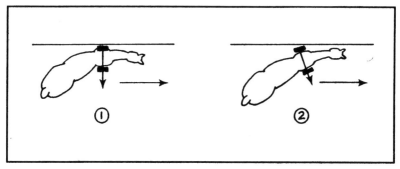

Fig. 59 - 1 = haunches-in (theoretical). Shoulders stay square to movement. 2 = haunches-in (real). Due to the absence of collar bone, inside shoulder is somewhat free to move ahead in order to alleviate the constraint brought about by bending. So, "haunches-in" is practically a fourth name for the same movement!

Half-Pass, Travers, Renvers, Haunches-In

These are all the same movement, with different titles. Travers is a half-pass head to the wall. Renvers is the same, but croup to the wall. Half-pass is supposed to be performed on a more or less diagonal line.

Imagine that you are in a desert, on your horse, with no judge in sight, performing a half-pass *(Fig. 57)*. You can call it a "travers" if you imagine a wall in front of you, parallel to your direction of march (there are mirages in a desert; it's a well-known fact). You can call it "renvers" if you imagine the wall behind you, or a "half-pass" if you arrange the walls differently in your mind. Still, the movement has not been modified a jot *(Fig. 58)*.

As *concerns haunches-in* on the track, it could be objected that, in this latter movement, the shoulders of a horse remain square to the direction of march, the lateral component featuring only with the haunches. This is true, in theory. In fact, due to the absence of bone-to-bone connection between the shoulders and the spine, which gives the former a relative liberty, the shoulder line does not remain perpendicular to the spine when a horse is bent. Therefore, this line displays some obliquity with respect to the direction of march, which equates the movement to a travers *(Fig. 59)*.

Shoulders Preceding the Haunches in a Lateral Movement

This is a totally cosmetic requirement, which does not have any connection with the movement itself, for when the judge (or whoever) sees the haunches of your horse ahead of the shoulders, it is only because he (or she) is placed at a given spot in space. Would he (or she) have been one or two feet more to the right or to the left, his (or her) perspective would have been different, and a movement heretofore considered "incorrect" would then look "correct" *(Fig. 60 and 61)*.

One more time, imagine yourself in a desert, performing a half-pass, in the absence of any witness, wall, "line in the sand," etc. How can you tell that "the haunches have preceded the shoulders?" There is no way, unless the angle of movement has exceeded 90 degrees, making your horse *back up in his lateral movement* (which is what this notion meant, when it was put forth in the baroque riding era). So you have 90 degrees of margin in the obliquity of your half-pass before this "danger" is met. Relax! *(Fig. 62)*

Yet this notion, although completely cosmetic as concerns the value

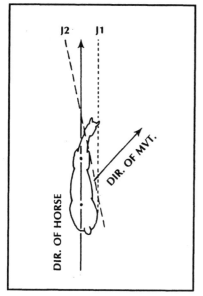

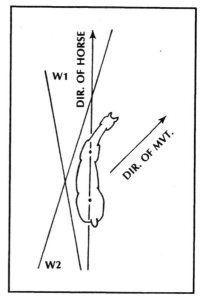

Fig. 60 - Now we are still in the desert, but we have brought a judge. If we place him at J1, he will see the haunches first and will say "bad." Yet, if we place him at J2, he will see the shoulders first and will say "good." But could a movement be both bad and good good?

Fig. 61 - So let's drop the judge, and trace a line in the sand representing the wall of an imaginary arena. If the wall is W1, the half-pass is "good." Yet, if the wall is at W2, the movement is wrong. But can a movement be both correct and incorrect?

This shows that the requirement for the shoulders to go "ahead of the haunches" in a half-pass is totally cosmetic, since its fulfillment depends entirely upon arbitrary and external factors: position of a judge, or direction of a wall.

of the movement in itself, keeps a marginal utility by forcing the rider, in a show, to *control the obliquity of the movement* and not let the horse take the obliquity he pleases.

But, when you work alone, be aware that as long as the obliquity of movement does not exceed 90 degrees (side-pass of the western riding), the haunches *DO NOT* precede the shoulders.

Performed on a circle, a half-pass brings the haunches of the horse within the circle (for instance, half-pass to right on a circle clockwise). This is nothing else than haunches-in on a circle. If the direction of movement

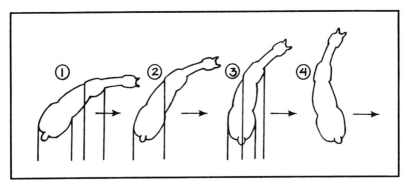

*Fig. 62 - Half-pass: True meaning of the requirement for the haunches not to go ahead of the shoulders. Here is a horse in half-pass whose angle grows steadily bigger, and yet it is only with the position **4** that one can say that the haunches are fully going ahead of the shoulders, since the horse "backs up laterally." In position **1** both shoulders preceed both haunches with respect to the direction of the movement. In position **2** the outside shoulder is caught up with the inside haunch; they are both on the same line in respect to the movement. In position **3** the inside haunch has passed the outside shoulder, with respect to the movement. Still, the inside shoulder keeps ahead of the inside haunch.*

on the circle is opposite to the direction of the half-pass (half-pass to right on a circle counter-clockwise), the haunches of the horse go outside of the circle. This is nothing else than haunches-out on a circle.

By diminishing progressively the radius of the circle, haunches-in tends toward the "pirouette," and haunches-out toward the "reversed pirouette" *(Fig. 63 & 64).*

VII. Halt, Half-Halt

Halt and half-halt are two of the three exercises performed on a straight line which La Guérinière recommends for improving collection (reining back is the third).

Halt

By halt, one must understand a stopping process which does not utilize the descending gamut of the gaits: it is a steep halt, from a canter or a trot. In the baroque era, this exercise bore the name of "parade," from

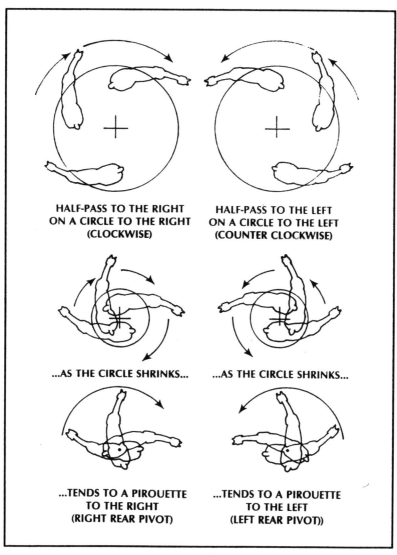

HALF-PASS TO THE RIGHT ON A CIRCLE TO THE RIGHT (CLOCKWISE)

HALF-PASS TO THE LEFT ON A CIRCLE TO THE LEFT (COUNTER CLOCKWISE)

...AS THE CIRCLE SHRINKS...

...AS THE CIRCLE SHRINKS...

...TENDS TO A PIROUETTE TO THE RIGHT (RIGHT REAR PIVOT)

...TENDS TO A PIROUETTE TO THE LEFT (LEFT REAR PIVOT))

Fig. 63

the Spanish word "parrar" which means "to stop." The German riders have kept the word.

To stop and, under the circumstances, to stop suddenly, almost brutally, a horse must indeed brace his back, lower his croup, and engage considerably his hind legs; in other words, "over collect" himself.

[87]

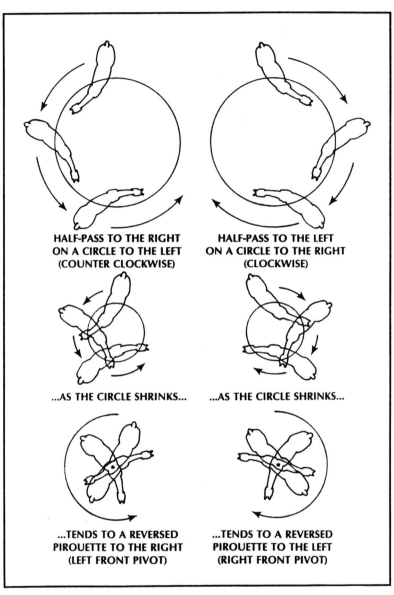

HALF-PASS TO THE RIGHT
ON A CIRCLE TO THE LEFT
(COUNTER CLOCKWISE)

HALF-PASS TO THE LEFT
ON A CIRCLE TO THE RIGHT
(CLOCKWISE)

...AS THE CIRCLE SHRINKS...

...AS THE CIRCLE SHRINKS...

...TENDS TO A REVERSED
PIROUETTE TO THE RIGHT
(LEFT FRONT PIVOT)

...TENDS TO A REVERSED
PIROUETTE TO THE LEFT
(RIGHT FRONT PIVOT)

Fig. 64

A perfect halt, especially from a canter, can only result from specific training. The exercise should not be asked for too often, or too prematurely, lest one impair the horse's generosity.

[88]

Exercise

Horse mouthed with snaffle. Canter in a "two point" position. Shorten considerably one rein, then set the hand which holds this rein on the horse's crest, firmly **pushing onto the crest**, although the rein should remain taut. When this base is assured, pull briskly with the other rein, rather upwards. The action must be lightning sharp, very strong, but very, very short, and possibly repeated, in rhythm with the canter.

Usually this action stops the canter in two or three strides, without any intermediate strides of trot or walk. Note that the gait stops completely as this pulsated action is in a phase of "release."

The secret lies in the total passivity of the other hand. For whichever reason, many riders do not seem capable of avoiding to pull, ever so slightly, with this passive hand because they cannot *FIX* it. This proceeds from the old reflex of "balancing off the reins." So, in the beginning, have somebody from the ground watch this hand carefully and tell you if it has moved (incorrect) or not (correct).

When the horse is accustomed to this way of stopping, use the same procedure, but in a more seated position and with longer reins, until the moment when only the fact of "suggesting" the action will get the horse's attention and bring about the desired result with a much lesser expense of strength.

Half-Halt

Still, this exercise remains very difficult to perform correctly, and very tiring for the horse. This is why La Guérinière invented the "half-halt" which, he says "may be repeated often without breaking the gait of a horse" (op. cit. p. 190).

As a matter of fact, in a half-halt, the notion of "halt," (i.e., of slowing) is secondary. The primary goal is to obtain the same benefit on the balance and collection of the horse as those drawn from a halt, without interrupting the movement.

In fact, in the French Horsemanship, a half-halt does not modify the speed. Hence, it can even be performed at a halt.

The half-halt is practiced with one rein or both (but, in this case, alternately), on the snaffle or on the curb. It should give the rider the impression one has when one is lifting a somewhat heavy stone from a step, in a staircase, in order to set it down delicately onto the next step.

The half-halt is always followed by a release of hands. The legs may

[89]

intervene, but compulsorily after this release of hands (i.e., after the half-halt has been completed).

The half-halt is essential to maintain the balance in a canter with a horse who has still not reached the capability of "self-collection," but it should never be obtrusive.

The half-halt is a procedure of training whose necessity decreases as the training progresses. When a horse is fully schooled, the half-halt is no longer necessary.

VIII. Flexion of Jaw

This is the centerpiece of riding in lightness, and what separates it fundamentally from the riding of German Tradition, now enforced in the dressage ring.

The flexion, or rather, *yielding* of the lower jaw, upon request from the rider, to the half-tension of one rein, or both reins, is the sign that the mouth is not the setting of unnecessary contractions. The relaxation of the lower jaw propagates to the whole front end of the horse, which is the area most perturbed by the rider's weight.

The yielding of the lower jaw involves a whole, very specific process, which starts with the opening of the mouth, continues with an up-and-down movement of the tongue under the bits (which makes them "jingle," as if the horse were swallowing his saliva), and ends with the shutting of the mouth.

The yielding of the jaw is not any "chomping on the bit," which may express only the irritation, nervousness, or soreness of the horse's mouth. In the yielding of the jaw, the horse must momentarily *interrupt the contact with the bit, but with such a suppleness that this interruption comes as a proof of acceptance of the bit*, since it is immediately followed by a supple shutting of the mouth. *Any gaping of the mouth is NOT a sign of yielding; it is a sign of contraction.*

When this yielding happens, the rider cannot be mistaken; he or she has the impression that the horse's mouth literally melts in his or her fingers.

This "melting" of the jaw has always been the sign that a horse was in a total state of relaxation, hence, balance. Baucher's streak of genius was, by obtaining separately and almost artificially the *SIGN*, to foster the general conditions of balance which justify the said sign, if only for a very short duration.

Using the flexion of the lower jaw is a "feed back" technique. Its repetition brings about the repetition of these instants of "state of grace," and entails the creation of a permanent state of balance with the horse.

Fixed Hand

The last words of Baucher when he was dying were reported by General L'Hotte in *"Un officier de Cavalerie"* ("A Cavalry Officer," 1905): "...Then taking my hand and giving it the position of the 'hand of curb'..." (*the left hand, which in the past was holding both reins of curb:* author), "he said: 'remember, always this' - and he immobilized my hand under the pressure of his - 'never that,' and he pulled my hand toward his chest."

One is allowed to think that, on the brink of passing away, Baucher wanted to sum up all his methods by pointing out the most important of his teachings — the "fixed hand."

The fixed hand is not a hand which refuses to follow the useful movements of the horse's mouth. It is a hand which in demanding a flexion of jaw, *fixes itself* so as to avoid any movement of "recoil" upon the horse's yielding to it.

It is realized by a pressure of the fist on the rein, without any help from any arm traction. Simply stated, it is the action which one uses in order to crush a lump of dirt, and not the action one uses to open a drawer.

Since there is no recoil at all, yielding, for the horse, becomes "self-rewarding," and will therefore tend to become easier and easier.

How to Ask for Flexion of Jaw

In the beginning, it may be advisable to start from the ground, since in this way the rider can observe the horse's mouth and make fruitful associations between what he sees and what he feels in his fingers. Subsequently, he will be more capable of interpreting his sensations while on horseback, where he cannot see the mouth.

But this technique also offers a shortcoming, which is that it is more difficult, from the ground, to avoid "pulling," (i.e., using some kind of arm traction). This is why, as soon as possible, the flexion of jaw will be asked for from horseback. The best way is to start with a counted walk, where soft, spontaneous flexions of jaw are likely to happen.

However, the flexion of jaw requires some tact. In the beginning, errors are almost inevitable. The snag lies in the temptation of "pulling," that is, using more or less a traction from the arms, in which case the horse will either fight or become aggravated and grind his teeth, or make them clatter, etc.

As a matter of fact, a rider can hardly understand the technique out of the mere reading of a book, and almost compulsorily has to be initiated to it by an instructor who, himself or herself, is versed in this type of horsemanship.

Nevertheless, there is an infallible way to know if one is "pulling" — upon the horse's yielding, if the rider's hand displays any "recoil," the rider was pulling.

Prior to the action, the tight adjustment of the reins is of utmost importance. Clenching the fist on the reins has no intrinsic virtue; it draws all its power from the previous adjustment of the reins. Squeezing the reins in place (clenching the fist) is the way to increase the pressure on the bit *without using any arm traction* (i.e., avoiding any recoil with the hand upon completion of the flexion).

In the event the flexion is slow to come about, although all of the above was being fully implemented, the rider has two possibilities left:

1) *Release the action.* Many a time, the flexion appears exactly as the rider begins to soften his or her action, which means that, unconsciously, he or she was "pulling," and that the horse was aware of it.

It is probably this phenomenon which had led Baucher to prescribe "vibrations" with the hands in order to obtain the relaxation of the jaw, since a vibration includes, in equal parts, tractions and releases. Yet the vibration should not become the usual way to obtain flexions of jaw.

2) *Use of the spur.* As the hand keeps its pressure, use the spur through a "delicate pinching" or through "little attacks" (see Section XI; **The Spur**). Release the action of spur as the flexion comes about.

Flexion of Jaw and Impulsion

On occasion of a trip to Germany, Baucher was reproached by some German officers that his horses were "behind the bit." At first, Baucher was surprised by this remark, but then he retorted, "I want it to be so, I want my horses behind the bit and ahead of the legs." And, of course, if a horse is "ahead of the legs," he cannot be "behind the bit," no matter the tension with the reins.

But there is more: the relaxation of the jaw *increases the horse's sensitivity to the rider's legs*, as stands out from these two experiments:

First experiment: As a horse is in his stall, try to push his croup sideways by applying a thrust on his hip; he more than likely will refuse to move, pushing in turn against your hand.

Then ask someone to introduce one finger in the horse's mouth, and kind of play with his tongue. There will come a moment when the horse will give a rudimentary flexion of jaw, and, at this very moment, if you have continued to apply a push on the horse's hip, *this push will suddenly go through with ease.*

Second experiment: Take a horse who has not received any specific training to the single leg. Equip this horse with a full bridle, which is more likely to provoke flexions of jaw. Mount the horse, stop him in the middle of the arena and, using a single leg, ask him to move his croup sideways. He more than likely will refuse.

Then try to get a flexion of jaw, and in the fraction of a second that follows, use the single leg. The horse will obey it.

Flexion of Jaw and "Ramener"

Theoretically, the jaw flexion should not entail any movement with the head. Nevertheless, if the jaw flexion brings about a flexion at the poll, *without lowering of the top of the head*, one should be satisfied, since the final result was reached in one stroke.

Most of the time, however, the "ramener" comes as an indirect result of the flexion; the jaw flexion creates the best possible conditions for the conquest of collection which, in turn, perfects the head set (see Section IX, **Impulsive Flexion**).

In order to accelerate the appearance of the "ramener," one may practice the following exercise:

Exercise

At a halt, lift the head as high as possible, with the forehead horizontal. Ask for a flexion of jaw (surprisingly, it is easy in this attitude). Then set your hands down, let the head take its place by lengthening slightly the reins, and complete the ramener through soft and alternate pressures of the fingers.

Then, try to walk, keeping the ramener. If the ramener deteriorates, stop and redo the whole maneuver.

The same from walk to trot, etc.

[93]

IX. Impulsive Flexion

The impulsive flexion is a technique combining the relaxation of the jaw and the forward movement, so as to replace the couple "action - contraction," which is the rule with an untrained horse, with the couple "relaxation - action."

It consists of demanding systematically an increase in the frame of the action, each time that one has obtained a flexion of jaw. In time, a reflex will be created by which the horse, each time that he has yielded in his jaw, will tend to extend his gait on his own, *without the help of the rider's leg.*

Already moving in a self-impulsion, through the systematic implementation of the principle of release of aids, the horse now learns how to increase this impulsion each time he has given a jaw flexion. This is a superior form of release of aids; the legs are not engaged, and yet the horse is in a high degree of impulsion.

The rider's legs hence remain available FOR STILL MORE, and the realm of "High School" movements is within reach of the rider.

Exercises

1) Halt. Flexion of jaw, departure into walk.

2) Halt. Flexion of jaw, departure into trot.

3) Halt. Flexion of jaw, departure into canter.

4) Walk. Flexion of jaw, departure into trot.

5) Walk. Flexion of jaw, departure into canter.

6) Medium Trot. Flexion of jaw, extended trot.

Remarks:

1) In the down transitions, try to avoid the flexions of jaw, since the horse has been conditioned to an *increase* of action upon producing them.

2) To slow a horse, the action is "pulsated," and produced by the back of the rider, the hands being only the point of insertion of the reins onto the rider's torso.

To get a flexion of jaw, the hand is contracted on the reins in a plain and not pulsated action, which may last more than one-half second, depending on the immediateness of the horse's response.

So these two actions should not be mistaken by the horse.

Remark: It is advisable to ask for the flexion only with the curb, in order to use the snaffle each time that the jaw flexion (which, after this specific training, has become impulsive) is not wished; for instance at a halt.

X. "Effet d'ensemble"

"Effet d'ensemble" is an expression of the Baucherist method whose simplest translation would be "effect on the whole of the horse."

It is used to overcome a fighting horse, or to teach a horse not to raise his head upon the rider's leg pressure. Since it is practiced with spurs, it requires some riding experience and is not within the reach of the novice rider.

How to Implement It

At a halt, apply progressively the legs, and resist with the hands accordingly, in order to prevent the horse from moving forward. As soon as possible, come to skin contact with the spurs, and press them very progressively, without jabbing. The spurs must come together to skin contact and work by "pinching." It is the critical moment when the horse's reactions may be very strong and dangerous. But as soon as the spurs apply frankly and calmly, any brusque reaction from the horse is ruled out; the spurs have an "inhibitive" effect which somewhat paralyses the horse.

Then press stronger and stronger. Don't release the hands, although their opposition is no longer necessary. The horse will round his frame, engage his hindquarters, generally heave a sigh, and give the rider an impression of total surrendering. Give immediately with hands, spurs, and legs.

Remarks:

1) The "effet d'ensemble" is the sheer denial of the principle of separation of aids, though the contradiction is lesser than it seems, because it comes about only in the start, when the legs - but not the spurs - squeeze the horse's sides. As soon as the spurs come to contact, they act as inhibitors by their pinching (see Section XI; **The Spurs**) and their action does not oppose that of the hands, but complements it.

Still, the "effet d'ensemble" should only be used occasionally, to dominate a very difficult horse, or to fight a particular stiffness at the poll.

2) The "effet d'ensemble" can be performed at slow gaits. The speed should remain unchanged (very difficult). *It is most important to practice an immediate release of the aids, as the effet d'ensemble is*

[95]

completed.

3) The "effet d'ensemble" brings generally a flexion of jaw. *Yet this is not its purpose.* If one chooses, as advised in this book, to commit the flexion of jaw to the curb, the "effet d'ensemble" should be practiced with the snaffle.

4) Collection is not the goal of the "effet d'ensemble," though if the horse gives a flexion of jaw upon yielding to the "effet d'ensemble," and if he has been more or less schooled in the impulsive flexion, the "effet d'ensemble" becomes a tool of collection.

5) Theoretically, the "effet d'ensemble" calms and regularizes the gaits, whereas collection animates and overexcites the horse. Collection is sought through *alternate* actions of hands and legs, mostly by means of impulsive flexions.

6) Pushing steadily onto the bit at a steady gait, as in the German way, has nothing to do with the "effet d'ensemble."

The "effet d'ensemble:"

    a) is occasional;

    b) creates lightness;

    c) is followed by a total and immediate release of aids.

As a matter of fact, the "half-halt" as practiced by the modern German horsemanship, is the closest to the Baucherist "effet d'ensemble."

A very practical type of "effet d'ensemble:" At the halt, use the reins first, as explained in Section VII (**Halt, Half-Halt**), by shortening a rein, fixing the corresponding hand on the crest, and pulling upwards with the other rein. Prevent the backing up that this action should create, with an action of spurs (constant and strong pinching). If, nevertheless, the horse backs up, practice an "opening rein" with the rein which pulls, in order to make the horse turn (it is more difficult for a horse to back up if he also has to turn).

This is very educational for horses with an incorrect head set

XI. The Spur

Spurs can be wielded in four different ways:

1) Soft pinching ("delicate pinching by the spurs," Antoine de Pluvinel, riding teacher of King Louis XIII, 1555-1620);

2) Strong pinching;

3) Soft pricking ("small attacks," Baucher, 1796-1873);

4) Stabbing ("full attacks," Baucher).

The first two (pinchings) are inhibitive and, somehow, relaxing. The last two (attacks) are impulsive.

In the pinching action, the whole neck of the spur is applied as evenly as possible on the horse's side, as the rowel (or edge) plays but a small role.

Soft pinching is used to start or restart a rein back (see Section XII). It is also used to foster the appearance of a flexion of jaw which lingers to come about. In this latter case, it is just a reinforcement means, it is not the usual way to ask for a jaw flexion.

Strong pinching is used in the "effet d'ensemble." Small attacks are used to arouse the horse's activity, or to trigger off the rein back in the event the soft pinching is not being efficient.

Full attacks were used by Baucher in his first manner, which was more forceful than his second, in order to "enclose" a horse between curb and spurs, as a means to obtain an extreme of collection. Implemented by an experienced rider who knows what he is doing and what he is looking for, they may be a good schooling tool, but in any other case they come more as a mere punishment.

When making attacks, whether small or full, do not remove the calves from the horse's sides.

XII. Rein Back

1) *With a horse that flexes freely his lower jaw:* Halt. Ask for a deep flexion of jaw, whereupon pull very softly onto one rein. The horse will rein back, the diagonal on the side of the acting rein moving first.

2) *If this does not work, for lack of relaxation with the horse:* Halt. Apply a traction with the hands, enough to make the horse understand that something is in process, but not enough to pull out the movement by sheer force. Then apply the spurs, through a soft pinching (preferably), or a soft poking. This is likely to trigger off the backing up.

As the horse starts reining back, release the spurs and legs, keep a soft tension with the reins. This tension may be "pulsated," with each back step. If the backing up stops, *do not increase the tension with the reins*, but come one more time with the spurs as you did to start the movement.

Shoulders back, and if necessary, legs to stop the backing up movement.

[97]

3) *With a horse that resists the two previous ways:* Move forward, then laterally, and then try to inflex the lateral movement backwards. In other words, try to voluntarily commit the error which consists of moving back as you go sideways. When the movement begins to go rearways, straighten it up. Be very progressive.

4) *With a horse who rears upon being asked to back up:* Come with the spurs on both sides *at the very same time* and, if possible, when the rearing is at its acme, then pinch more and more strongly. This inhibits the normal play of the muscles on the sides of the horse, impairs his coming back down to the ground, which he does slowly and with pain. When on the ground, continue the use of spurs joined to an action of hands, as for an "effet d'ensemble."

The horse will rapidly learn how not to rear when asked for a backing up. Resume the exercise as described here above, in paragraph (2).

5) *From the ground:* Face the horse, then take each ring of snaffle with thumbs, push calmly forward (i.e., rearward for the horse) and *upwards.* As the horse backs up, make sure that he does not dissociate his diagonals. This requires tact.

Also, release the hand action as soon as the horse moves back, and "pulsate," in rhythm with the movement.

Important Remarks

When backing up a horse from the saddle:

1) *Never move your hands closer to your body.* In other words, do not pull with arms, but with your back.

2) Still, do not overdo the withdrawal of your shoulders, since it should foster a forward movement with the horse, and hence come across the desired result.

3) Avoid, by all means, any split in the diagonals. The main interest of reining back is the tipping under of the pelvic bone. It happens only when the diagonal character of the movement is present.

XIII. Departures into Canter

Departures into canter from a rein back, a halt, or a slow trot are a very good schooling to collection.

It is also very profitable to link the departure into canter to any kind of lateral movement, to benefit from the setting onto the haunches these movements provide.

With this respect, twelve exercises (six for each direction) may be

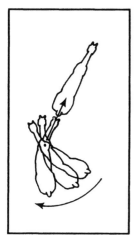 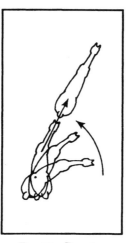 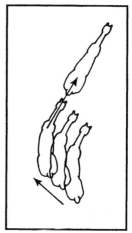

Fig. 65 - Turning around shoulders to the left (horse bent to the right). Depart canter on right lead.

Fig. 66 - Turning around haunches to the left (horse bent to the right). Depart canter on right lead.

Fig. 67 - Right shoulder-in. Horse moves to the left (bent to the right). Depart canter on right lead.

envisaged:

Exercises

1) (right rein) Turning around shoulders to left at a walk (horse bent to right), followed with a departure into canter right lead *(Fig. 65)*.

2) (right rein) Turning around haunches to left at a walk (horse bent to right), followed with a departure into canter right lead *(Fig. 66)*.

3) (right rein) Right shoulder-in at a walk (horse bent to right, moving laterally to left), followed with a departure into canter right lead *(Fig. 67)*.

4) (right rein) Reversed pirouette to right at a walk (horse bent to right, croup turning to right around shoulders), followed with a departure into canter right lead *(Fig. 68)*.

5) (right rein) Pirouette to right at a walk (horse bent to right, shoulders turning to right around haunches), followed with a departure into canter right lead *(Fig. 69)*.

6) (right rein) Half-pass to right (horse bent to right, moving laterally to right), followed with a departure into canter right lead *(Fig. 70)*.

7) to 12) (left rein) Same as exercises #1 through #6, left rein, canter left lead.

[99]

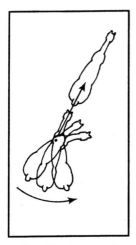 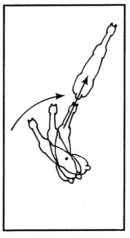 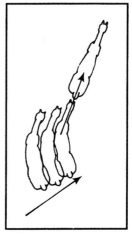

Fig. 68 - Reversed
pirouette to the right.
Depart canter on right
lead.

Fig. 69 - Pirouette to
the right. Depart can-
ter on the right lead.

Fig. 70 - Half-pass to
the right. Depart can-
ter on the right lead.

Remarks:

1) The canter is not lateral. It is straight, and taken in the direction of the horse's body on his lateral movement. The canter marks the end of the lateral movement. The canter is in one direction, the lateral movement is in another. The angle defined by these two directions is the angle of the initial lateral movement.

2) Ask for canter with the outside leg, as the outside front foot of the horse is on the ground (use the inside leg in exercise #4).

3) Turning around haunches (exercise #2) should be performed with marked bending. Give with the inside rein in order to straighten up the horse as you start the canter.

4) Turning around shoulders (exercise #1) should be performed with a very slim bending, if any.

5) Exercises #2 and #4 are the most productive.

PART FOUR

High School

I. Mechanism of the Gaits

Walk

Walk is a four beat gait. Since it does not display any suspension time, it is a "crawled" gait, which means that there is always at least one foot of the horse on the ground. As a matter of fact, as he walks, a horse always has at least two, and at the maximum, three feet on the ground.

At a walk, the base of support of a horse evolves between a tripod and a bipod which is alternately diagonal and lateral.

To be more descriptive, let's imagine a horse who starts walking by reaching out first with the right front leg. During a short period, he rests on a tripodal base, made of the left front leg and the two rear legs. Then, before he sets his right fore down on the ground, he lifts the left rear; he thus is on a bipedal base, which is the left diagonal. When the right fore grounds, the base becomes tripodal again, as it is comprised with the two front legs and the right hind leg. Then the left fore quits the ground and the base becomes bipedal again, but this time in a lateral way, since the two members on the ground are those of the right lateral. Then the left hind leg sets down in turn and the base turns again to a tripod right front and two rear. Then, the right rear rises, and the base is bipedal anew, as it is comprised with the right diagonal. Then the left front sets down and the base turns one more time to a tripod, comprised with the two front feet and the left rear. Then the right front foot rises, and the base is now bipedal, as it is assured by the left lateral, etc. (*Fig. 71*).

It is to be noticed that:

1) After the *grounding of a rear foot,* and for the duration of about a half step, the horse stands on a *diagonal* (right diagonal after the

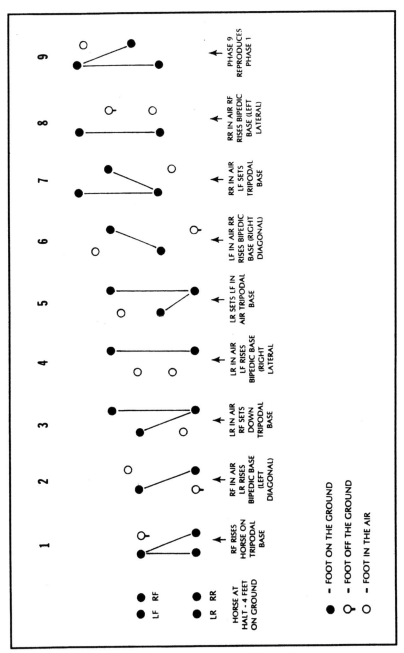

Fig. 71 - The eight phases of the walk.

grounding of left rear, and vice-versa), and;

2) After the *grounding of a fore foot*, and for the same duration of about a half step, the horse stands on a *lateral* (the lateral of the side of the front foot which has set down).

This pattern of systematic modification of the base of support in a walk may be taken advantage of by the rider in the timing of his/her demands for transitions. For instance, if the rider's left leg acts immediately after the left hind leg of the horse has set down, the horse is more likely to start a trot than a canter, since at this very moment, the base becomes diagonal.

On the other hand, if the rider's left leg acts immediately after the left front leg of the horse has set down, canter is more likely to come about, since the horse at this very moment is on a lateral base.

Particular emphasis should also be set upon the order in which the feet set down on the ground in a walk. This order is:

left rear...left front...right rear...right front...

If we take as origin for the sequence, the grounding of a rear foot - the left one, under the circumstances - walk appears as a lateral gait whose laterals are dissociated. In effect, two members of the same lateral biped set down first (left rear, left front), then the two members of the other lateral (right rear, right front). But they don't set down together; the laterals are dissociated to the advantage, so to speak, of the rear foot, which sets down first.

But, if we take as origin for the sequence, a front foot (say, the left front), the sequence reads as follows:

left front...right rear...right front...left rear...

It now looks as if walk were a diagonal gait, whose diagonals are dissociated. In effect, two members of a same diagonal, the left one under the circumstances (left front, right rear) sets down first, then the two members of the other diagonal (right front, left rear). But the dissociation of the diagonals operates now to the advantage, so to speak, of the front foot, which sets down first.

This is not idle talk because it shows that, depending on the *rhythm* of the walk, a lateral or a diagonal character may evidence more particularly. If, for instance, two members of the same lateral set down rapidly one after another, the walk tends to be *lateral* (at the limit, if they would set down simultaneously, the horse would "amble"). If two members of the same diagonal would set down rapidly one after another, the walk would take a *diagonal* character (at the limit, if they would set down simultaneously, the horse would "jog").

It will be noticed that, as the interval of time separating the grounding of two members of a same pair, lateral or diagonal, diminishes, the duration of support of the horse by this same pair augments. In other words, in a "lateral" walk, the two members of the same lateral tend to set down more rapidly one after the other than do the two members of a diagonal, but the horse remains longer on his laterals than he does on his diagonals.

This explains why a "direct accompanying" with the hands, of the grounding of the front hooves, tends to *lateralize* the walk, since it tends to lengthen the duration of the support on a lateral, by bringing the weight on this lateral (which becomes the only base of support as long as the diagonally opposed rear foot has not set down).

Likewise, a cross-accompanying with the hands of the grounding of the front feet will tend to *diagonalize* the walk, since it will tend to withhold the grounding of the other front foot, delaying its grounding and hence shortening the interval of time separating this grounding from that of the diagonally-opposed rear foot.

It is to be noticed that the rhythm of a medium walk is even - neither diagonal nor lateral - the rhythm of an accelerated free walk is lateral, and the rhythm of a slowed walk tends to be diagonal. It should be noted, also, that certain breeds (Lipizzans, Andalusians, Quarter Horses) evince more aptitude for diagonalizing the walk than others.

Trot

Trot is a two-beat, diagonally jumped gait. The diagonals are no longer dissociated as in a walk; they remain united and their grounding is followed with a suspension time during which a horse has *no feet on the ground*. In other words, in a trot, a horse jumps from one diagonal to the other.

In a "jog," the suspension time disappears or is unnoticeable; it amounts to a diagonal walk. Many horses, more particularly Arabians, Thoroughbreds or their relatives, tend to display a "semi-jog," that is, they walk in front and trot behind. The Andalusian breed evince the reverse shortcoming; they trot in front and walk behind.

As a matter of fact, there are not many horses who trot "correctly." Let alone the possible character of "semi-jogging" mentioned above, they almost all trot in four beats, even if most of the time unnoticeably. In effect, the diagonals remain slightly dissociated, the *front foot coming systematically a tad sooner onto the ground than the diagonally opposed rear foot.*

This fact is difficult to diagnose, since many photographs of trotters in action show horses whose extending front foot seems farther from the ground than the extending rear. This is due to the difference in shape, in a trot, between the leg gesture in front and behind. But the vivacity of the front legs' movement makes up for this difference, and in fact, the front foot touches the ground invariably, if ever so slightly, *before* its diagonally opposed counterpart.

And this brings forth a surprising conclusion which is that, *in fact*, the sequence of hooves grounding in a trot is *similar* to that of a walk; that is,

left front…right rear…right front…left rear.

But this is to be taken with a grain of salt, since let alone the fact that a trot is "jumped" whereas a walk is not, the *rhythm* is also completely different, due to the very short, and most often unnoticeable, interval appearing between the two beats of a same diagonal.

Still, this explains why a direct accompanying, with the hands of the grounding of the front feet, will provoke an easy transition to walk *since it has the same lateralizing properties as if implemented at a walk.*

Canter

Canter is a three-beat, jumped gait, comprising only one time of suspension, which comes about after the third beat. In a natural, semi-collected canter, the interval between first and second beat is about one-sixth of the total duration of the stride; the interval between second and third beat is about a third of the total duration of the stride, and the suspension time occupies a half of the stride.

Acoustically, this third beat is easy to determine, since it is the last of a group of rather precipitated beats. Visually, it corresponds to the grounding of a front leg. The first beat corresponds to the grounding of the diagonally opposed rear foot, the second beat corresponds to the grounding of the two other feet, diagonally associated.

In other words, if the right rear marks the first beat, the right diagonal will mark the second beat and the left fore, the third beat. The canter is then called a left lead canter, since the left front leg is extended at the end of the sequence.

In a canter right lead, the left rear marks the first beat, the left diagonal marks the second and the right front marks the third.

An observation similar to that made for a trot can be made for a canter; it is that the second beat is not one hundred percent neat, it is slightly divided as the front foot tends to come a bit faster to the ground than its diagonal counterpart.

Therefore, the real sequence of the beats in a canter will *one more time reproduce that of a walk*. For example, in a canter right lead the sequence will be:

left rear…left front (slightly ahead of right rear)…right rear…right front

This is almost unnoticeable when the canter is "correct." But the four beats are neatly noticeable in a gallop, or even at a normal canter with certain horses (mostly gaited horses or trotters).

When a horse is excessively seated on the haunches, another form of four beat canter may occur, where the two rear feet set down *before* the two front feet. For instance, in a canter right lead, one will observe the following sequence:

left rear…right rear…left front…right front

This time, the second beat is dissociated to the advantage, so to speak, of the rear foot.

This type of canter, today considered as faulty, was in great regard in the baroque riding. It was called "galopade."

However, this latter type of four beat canter is *very rare*. When, for lack of impulsion, in a Dressage ring or elsewhere, a horse canters on four beats, it is almost always the first type of alteration described above which occurs.

Some books, sometimes written by experienced Dressage riders, equate the four beat gallop of the race tracks to a "galopade." This, of course, is totally irrelevant. Speed automatically sets a horse on the shoulders, and the split of the second beat happens mandatorily to the advantage, so to say, of the front foot.

Like the walk, canter presents a diagonal aspect and also a lateral aspect. Its diagonal feature proceeds from the association of a diagonal pair (the outside one) in the second beat of the gait. With this respect, one may describe a canter as a dissociated diagonal, which "frames," in its divided grounding, the grounding of the other, still united, diagonal. For instance, in a canter right lead the right diagonal is dissociated. Its first element (left rear) sets down first; then comes the second diagonal as a whole, in one beat; then comes the second element of the right diagonal, the right front foot.

But the lateral aspect is prevalent. In effect, in a canter right lead for instance, the left lateral (although divided) comes first to the ground, followed by the right lateral, also divided. If the canter is "correct," that is in three exact beats, the end of grounding of the outside lateral corresponds exactly to the beginning of grounding of the inside lateral. This instant is that of the second beat.

It is to be noted that the two laterals are animated with a similar pendulum movement, with the movement of the inside lateral slightly lagging, in time, behind the movement of the outside lateral.

Given its more advanced position in space, the inside lateral tends to position itself constantly ahead of the outside lateral. But given its lag, in its pendulum movement, behind the outside lateral, the inside lateral in its whole passes behind the outside lateral at the very end of the third beat (end of support of leading fore), and the very beginning of the suspension time.

This is the very best moment for the rider to demand, and the horse to execute, a flying change.

1) For the rider, since his/her seat is then oriented toward the new canter, his/her haunches following the movement of the laterals, right hip in motion with the right lateral, left hip in motion with the left lateral.

2) For the horse, since the flying change of lead is mandatorily produced *during the suspension time, as the horse has no feet on the ground and is one hundred percent free as concerns the gesture of his legs.*

II. School Walk

Very majestic walk, one of the most magnificent airs of High School. Start a counted walk, extend the gesture as much as possible without

[107]

accelerating the cadence, try to increase the diagonal character of the walk (very important). When the walk becomes really diagonal, the horse begins to "swim" with his front legs.

III. Spanish Walk

Can be obtained from the saddle. Halt. Ask for lightness in the mouth, then erect torso in the saddle, arch your back, push with the buttock bones. No legs; suggest a departure into walk, without really starting the walk; the horse will probably raise one fore leg (the right one, most often).

For the other front leg, the one which seems more reluctant to extend itself, ask for lightness at a halt, then use the crop over the shoulder until the horse lifts his arm. Reward by the first sign of willingness.

Ask often, be satisfied with little, reward much.

When a horse, upon being collected, extends his right front leg as the rider sits to the left, and lifts slightly his right hand, or symmetrically lifts his left leg as the rider sits to the right and slightly lifts his left hand, he is ready for the Spanish Walk.

To get it, extend one front leg, then let this front leg move forward and set down to the ground. Stop the horse and act in the same way with the other front leg, etc. In other words, combine the demands of elevation of the front legs with a normal slow walk.

IV. Extended Walk

Theoretically, when one accelerates the walk, the rhythm tends to lateralize.

The matter here is to keep an even tempo as one increases the length of the strides. So push, and in the meantime, cross-accompany with the hands, in order to "infuse" some diagonalization in the gait, to counter the lateralization.

V. Passage

Passage is a very slow, very cadenced, very elevated trot, with an important time of suspension. The strides should not exceed one foot in length.

At the maximum of their elevation, the forearms should be horizontal, the cannon hanging vertically. Gesture of the rear is less elevated, but must keep its "springing" feature (no stomping).

Passage is a natural gait, but a horse practices it rarely, only when he is excited, under the influence of a strong emotion.

When a horse is ready, it takes only ten minutes to teach him how to passage, but to get a horse ready may take a very long time, amounting to months, nay years.

Trying to make a horse passage, with forceful actions of legs, as he is still not ready for it, is only likely to jeopardize, if not totally suppress, the possibility of his passaging.

Passage must "blossom."

Here are a few exercises which may help accelerate the blossoming:
Exercises

1) Halt, impulsive flexion, trot.

2) Medium trot, impulsive flexion, extended trot. When the horse systematically extends his trot upon a flexion of jaw in a medium trot, *with no help of the legs at all*, he is ready for passage. Here is how to operate:

As the horse starts his extension, hold him back with the snaffle in order to direct *upwards* the impulsion created by the impulsive flexion. You may add an alternate action of legs, in unison with the grounding of the fore feet (right leg as right front foot hits the ground, left leg as the left front foot hits the ground), but *caution*; this leg action may well choke the dawning passage instead of fostering it.

Passage may also be obtained by a transition to trot from a Spanish Walk.

Often, also, after a horse has been worked in a collected canter and as the rider resumes trotting, the horse shows that he is ready to passage. Then the rider should softly *accompany* with the legs, the leg acting on the side of the front foot which sets down.

It is good to establish an association in the horse's mind between passage and this direct accompaniment from the legs, since it will then suffice to act in this way with the leg, as the horse is trotting, to automatically trigger the passage. But the horse should not "lean" onto this action of legs, and should constantly be left alone to passage on his own as soon as the passage has been started, no matter how.

VI. Piaffe

Piaffe is a trot in place. Depending on the importance of the suspension time in this trot, piaffe may become passage on place (very rare).

Piaffe is obtained by slowing down the trot to an extreme, without interrupting the gait, or by developing mobility on place.

A good way to slow the trot without breaking the gait is to trot more and more laterally, up to side-passing at a trot, and then to stop the lateral movement with the outside leg acting as the outside front foot hits the ground. This is likely to bring about one stride of piaffe.

Mobility on Place

1) *From a counted walk:* Slow down until walking in place. The walk becomes diagonal.

2) *From a halt:* Ask for lightness, then animate the horse with soft, alternate actions of legs.

3) *From a rein back:* Progressively slow the backing up movement by arching the back (no legs) and, when the horse is about to stop, come with soft alternate legs.

VII. Relation Between Piaffe and Passage

Although closely related, piaffe and passage are two different movements, and it is why the transition piaffe passage is so difficult, as long as the piaffe has not been perfected and promoted to the state of passage on place.

According to the impulsion contained in the piaffe, what one gets by moving forward from this air may be: a trot, a forward moving piaffe, or a passage. Natural passage is more than a forward moving piaffe; it requires more impulsion.

Yet passage is usually easier to get than piaffe, for it is less artificial, since the horse moves forward.

Piaffe by slowing down passage is sometimes very difficult to get, but so is natural passage by forwarding of piaffe, as many a time a horse taught how to piaffe first will simply resume trotting if, from the piaffe, he is required to move forward.

So much so that the schooling to both airs should be started simultaneously. Schooling to mobility in place can greatly help in the seeking to passage.

VIII. Collected Canter

Canter *is* a collected gait, so the expression "collected canter" is somewhat redundant. By "collected canter," we are pointing out here a very slow, although springing and sufficiently ample, canter.

This canter requires a very "silent," "neutral" seat (arching of the back). It is ridden in a *total release of the aids.* It can be obtained by starting a canter from a rein back, a halt, a walk ,or even a slow trot if, in this latter case, no increase in the speed is noticeable (ref. Part Three, Section III).

It is very important to check this canter as soon as it dawns. A very common error consists in omitting to monitor the canter by its incipience. The sooner this checking, the less conspicuous it will have to be. Lightness must remain unaltered. The rider must look for as slow but, in the meantime, as free a canter as possible. From time to time, the rider will stop, drop completely the reins (no contact with the hands whatsoever), wait a few seconds, and start a canter from a halt, without any intermediate stride of trot. Reins may be taken and adjusted (and the gait consequently checked) only as the horse canters.

IX. Half-Pass at a Canter

Easiness to move laterally is a proof that the canter is correctly seated on the haunches, but conversely, the schooling to half-pass at a canter can greatly improve the balance in this gait.

Cue to direct the movement laterally must come after the third beat of canter, in rhythm with the strides.

Counter bending (bending to right as the horse moves laterally to left, and vice versa) may be tolerated (and even indispensable) in the beginning.

If a horse resists, is reluctant to move laterally, first try to perfect lightness in the canter. If this does not suffice, drop suddenly the inside rein (the rein on the side toward which you try to move laterally), and force the horse to make a tight turn in the opposite direction. This punishment is very efficient, however, it is to be used with moderation.

X. Canter Pirouette

Weight must be kept to the outside, to prevent croup from moving outwards. Look (over your shoulder) in the direction of inside hip of the horse (Nuno Oliveira).

The FEI progression places the half-pirouette (180 degrees) before the full pirouette, as if the difficulty was to complete the pirouette. As a matter of fact, the difficulty lies in *limiting* the pirouette, since a horse, once engaged in a pirouette, tends to "fall" inside (which is a fault that may be tolerated in the beginning, then corrected further on).

Pirouette can be approached by cantering on two tracks on a circle whose diameter progressively diminishes.

Also, a very good approach consists in turning around the haunches at a trot. This movement is very difficult, and most of the time, in order to better balance themselves, horses will tend to spontaneously start a canter as they pirouette at a trot.

If the horse tends to "fall" into its pirouette, go on large circles haunches-in at a canter. Shorten progressively the diameter.

XI. "Terre-à-terre"

It is a two beat canter on two tracks. Slow the canter to an extreme as you half-pass; the cadence will modify itself and two beats will evince instead of three (at first, there will be four beats, the two rear feet first, then the two front feet, and later on the beats of a same pair, front or rear, will tend to come closer to each other).

XII. Single Flying Changes of Lead

Four conditions have to be realized:
    1) Horse must take his leads infallibly;
    2) Canter must display a specific quality;
    3) Specific timing must be respected;
    4) Horse must understand what is going on.

Infallibility of the Leads

The convention to establish firmly is that of the demand coming about, when the outside front foot is on the ground (canter from a trot or a walk).

Another convention links the lead to the bending (horse cantering right lead as he is bent to right). Although very useful, this latter convention comes second to the previous one.

Practice departures into canter in the most varied situations; for instance, start a counter-canter as you enter the corners of the arena (and this, regardless of the bending of the horse), etc. The horse must never be mistaken, miss his leads.

Quality of Canter

Natural canter is on three tracks (leading fore and outside rear on the same track). This canter must be straightened up, the croup placed in the alignment of the shoulders. It is safer to straighten the canter with the hands, the shoulders being brought in front of the haunches.

The time of suspension of the canter must be marked, but must proceed *upwards* rather than forwards. The upward movement of the croup by the end of the third beat (support of the horse's mass from the leading fore only) must be neatly felt by the rider.

To obtain this canter, try to slow the cadence as much as possible, whilst keeping the amplitude of the strides, by giving the neck the fullest extension possible.

Timing

The timing of demand may vary slightly depending on the horse, its degree of schooling, etc. However, one can take as a rule that the instant when to ask for the new canter is situated by the end of the third beat of canter, just before the suspension time.

At this very moment, the horse has only one foot on the ground (the leading fore), *the outside lateral is about to come ahead of the inside one for a very short period of time*, and the rider feels neatly his outside buttock lifted by the movement of the horse's croup. Visually, this corresponds to the forward movement of the outside shoulder.

Understanding from the Horse: Preliminary Exercises

1) A constant concern with the rider during all the schooling to canter will be to establish firmly a timing convention between him/her and the horse.

For this, ask for canter from a walk or trot *when the outside front foot of the horse is on the ground and comes back toward the rider* (forward movement of the inside shoulder).

This convention must be so firmly established as to prevail upon any

[113]

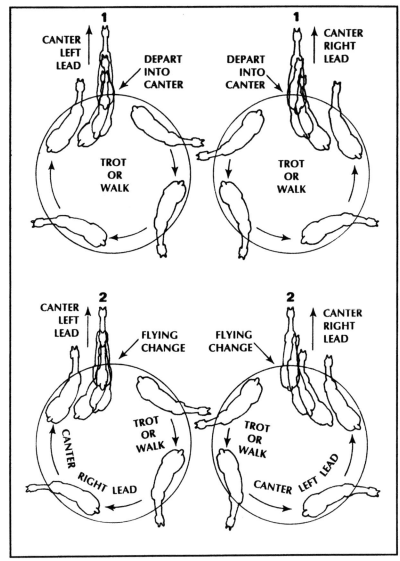

Fig. 72

possibly conflicting influence of bending, direction of work, etc.
2) Before asking for the first flying change, engage the horse in a counter shoulder-in, at a walk or trot (which works best), on a circle, and at a given point on this circle - always the same - start a canter

[114]

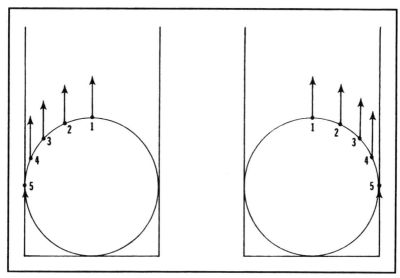

Fig. 73

Flying changes from right to left. Get them first in 1, then progressively in 2, 3, 4, and 5.

Flying changes from left to right. Get them first in 1, then progressively in 2, 3, 4, and 5.

straight forward, the demand coming when the outside front foot is coming back to the rider (forward movement of inside shoulder). Repeat until the horse is "mechanized" and jumps literally into its canter (*Fig. 72-1*).

Then, engage the horse one more time in a counter shoulder-in on a circle, but, as he walks or trots, use your inside leg (inside to the horse's curvature; i.e., left leg for a left counter shoulder-in) rhythmically with the grounding of the front leg on the same side, until the horse breaks into a canter, *nevertheless keeping its lateral movement* (that is, cantering right lead in a left shoulder-in, or vice versa). And, as you reach the point where the canter on the other lead has been demanded in the previous exercise from a walk or trot, ask for the new canter, *carefully respecting the timing* (that is, when the shoulder on the side of the new lead is moving forward) (*Fig. 72-2*).

Remarks:

1) In order to limit the possibilities of a flying change in two parts, the hind leg changing with a delay of one (if not more) stride with respect

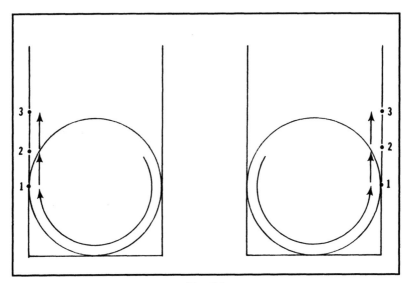

Fig. 74

Flying changes from the right to the left. Ask for it first at 1, then progressively at 2, after a short segment on a straight ne at 2, 3, etc.

Flying changes from the left to the right. Ask for it first at 1, then progressively at 2, after a short segment on a straight line at 2, 3, etc.

to the front legs, *carefully keep the haunches moving laterally up to the very moment of the demand.*

2) If the demand is made with the outside (outside with respect to the new canter) leg prevailing, first set this leg in a position neatly back from the girth, but direct its action *toward the diagonally opposite front leg* (new leading fore).

3) In this progression, the flying change is obtained upon a changing of direction as concerns the movement of the horse, but *with no changing of direction as concerns the horse's body.* This is very important.

To progressively tackle the flying changes on a straight line, the following exercises are recommended:

Exercises

   a) Counter shoulder-in at a trot or walk, at one extremity of the arena, on a circle whose diameter equals the width of the arena. Departure in the new canter at the point of intersection of this circle with the

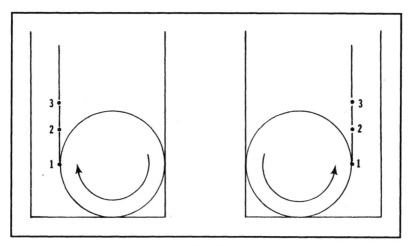

Fig. 75

Flying changes from right to left at
1, then 2, 3, etc.

Flying changes from left to right at
1, then 2, 3, etc.

middle line (*Fig. 72-1*).

b) Counter shoulder-in at a trot or walk in the same conditions as above, canter on the lead opposed to the horse's curvature, keeping the lateral movement. Flying change when crossing the middle line, new canter on the middle line (*Fig. 72-2*).

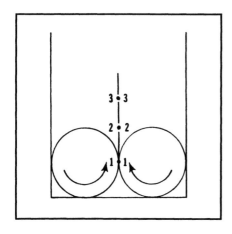

Fig. 76 - Flying changes from direct to counter-canter at 1, then 2, 3, etc.

c) Same counter shoulder-in and same canter on the same circle, but flying change asked sooner and sooner, closer and closer to the wall, up to changing from direct to counter-canter at the point of tangency of the circle with the wall (*Fig. 73*).

d) Flying change from direct to counter, at a point situated progressively farther along the wall (*Fig. 74*).

e) Canter direct lead in the end of arena, on a circle whose diameter equals three quarters of the small side. Engage on the quarter line. Flying change from direct to counter (*Fig. 75*).

f) Same exercise on the middle line, from both directions. The horse is schooled to flying changes on the straight line (*Fig. 76*).

XIII. "Tempi" Flying Changes

Immediately start the three stride flying changes. Horses know how to count up to three; they will tend to anticipate which, under the circumstances, is to be taken advantage of. Confirm the three stride flying changes especially on wide circles, or in the corners of the arena. Then start the two stride flying changes. Same exercises on wide circles.

Flying Changes at Every Stride

To be started only when the two stride flying changes are easy, light, lively, supple, happy...and straight.

Then take a lead, the right for instance, change to left and try to come back immediately to right. *Keep cantering right lead.* In other words, take a given lead, and interspersed scattered flying changes immediately "corrected" to come back to the lead of reference, as if it were about errors immediately straightened up.

Work in the same way on the other lead.

Then try two successive flying changes at every stride. For instance, like this:

- right, right, right, right, *left - right - left*, left, left, left, etc.

- left, left, left, left, *right - left - right*, right, right, right, etc.

Then try three successive flying changes at every stride. When a horse passes three successive flying changes at every stride, he is ready for longer sequences.

Remarks:

The two ticklish moments in a sequence of flying changes at every stride are the entry and the exit. The start and the end.

1) To start, it is advisable to slightly advance the timing of demand for the second flying change, and perhaps the third, whereafter the timing comes back to normal.

2) To get out of the series, without a horse repeating on his own and adding one or two unasked for flying changes, it is advisable to carry out the series on a diagonal and to quit as one reaches the opposite side of the arena.

Later on, quit at any given point inside of the arena, but upon a slight changing in direction, as if there were a wall. Then, of course, teach the horse how to interrupt the series when the rider's aids quit demanding, without using any longer these momentary subterfuges.

The author, piaffe, 1993

"NO-NOs"

1) **DO NOT** move your hand (hands) forward when you desire to "give," but *let the reins slide between your fingers.*

2) **DO NOT** keep your fingers clenched as you are using your legs. Open them.

3) **DO NOT** push for no result, ever. If you push, your horse *must* accelerate.

4) **DO NOT** come stronger (or kick) with the legs if the horse ignores them. *Add* the crop.

5) **DO NOT** resist with the hands for more than one half second at a time, *ever.*

6) **DO NOT** stiffen your elbows, *ever.* Keep them supple and bendable permanently. If your wrists "break" (if they are bent), it means that your elbows are *blocked.*

7) **DO NOT** remove your outside elbow far from your body in a bending movement (circle, shoulder-in, half-pass). Do not open it. Keep it one hundred percent symmetrical to the inside elbow (but don't forget, in the meantime, to give the outside rein more length, through an opening of your fingers).

8) **DO NOT** keep inside hand inside in a bending movement, but bring it toward the withers.

9) **DO NOT** move shoulders inside in a bending movement. Displacements of weight are displacements of seat; that is, of the mere pelvic bone.

Torso must remain upright over the pelvis in any circumstance.

10) **DO NOT** move the hand of the shortened rein as you teach a horse how to stop short at a canter. Set this hand down onto the crest, and *push it against the neck*, in order to avoid any back movement.

If the horse moves his head laterally upon your traction with the other rein, it means that the preparation with the shortened rein was wrong, too wishy-washy.

11) **DO NOT** ride with gloves (would you play the piano with gloves?).

12) **DO NOT** use braided reins, rubber reins, or any kind of coarse reins.

13) **DO NOT** *separate, ever, the tip of your thumbs from the reins.*

CONCLUSION

As the reader probably has realized, this book has exposed, on the one hand, a general philosophy and, on the other hand, a set of exercises, procedures, even some "tricks." But in the middle...no *progression*. Why?

Because, simply stated, there cannot be any rigidly fixed progression in High School training. Each horse, hence each training, is a particular case. For instance, I once had a horse who was already passaging whereas his canter was still pretty much lacking in balance. No wonder why: this horse was a French "trotter" (in the USA, he would have been called a "standardbred"). So, of course, he felt much less comfortable at a canter than at a trot.

Now the reader will ask, "Why on earth did you want to train a 'trotter' in High School?" My answer is, "Why not?" For the challenge in the first place; but, as a matter of fact, there was not that much of a challenge because, as it happens, riding in lightness *makes this type of prowess easy*.

Any horse, of whichever breed, provided he was normally strong and healthy, can be taught some part of the High School program, at least how to passage and how to pass flying changes every three, nay two strides. The secret (which is no longer a secret since you have read this book) lies in lightness. Lightness as a *systematic prerequisite to all your work* will rapidly give you collection, then self-collection, and then...*your horse himself will tell you what to ask from him.*

Collection is like the hat of the magician, from which one can pull a rose, then a shawl, then a rabbit, etc. But those marvelous things *never come in the same order*; a "galloper" will try to canter on place; an Andalusian will give you a piaffe first, or show no difficulty in performing pirouettes at a canter, which are so difficult for the warmbloods; an Anglo-Arab will exhibit a brilliant passage, etc. Some horses will show no difficulties at all for the flying changes of lead; others will be awkward in this particular matter.

[123]

The FEI places passage at the end of its progression, at the level of Grand Prix, whereas piaffe comes by the Intermédiare 2 and pirouette at a canter much earlier - by the level of Prix St. Georges. Now, experience shows that many horses can passage, but that much fewer can piaffe. So if you want to follow this progression, since you have decided to "show," and if, by any chance, your horse exhibits a real talent for passage, you will abstain from developing this talent, for fear of "wasting" your time.

Now, imagine that your horse shows some stubborn inability for the piaffe. He will be barred from the Intermédiare 2, let alone the Grand Prix. And here is a horse who will *never* be allowed to show how brilliant he can be in a passage!

It seems to me, in this very case, that the waste of time lies rather in showing. Waste of time, compounded with a waste of talent (for your horse).

I am, indeed, fully aware of the necessity for the FEI to have a progression; and, if they would in this case adopt the one I find more logical, other horses would be barred.

No, what I regret is that they have only one, based on a set of dogmas which our horses deny joyfully every day!

Now you will tell me that you want to perform in training level test one first, since you are a beginner and since training level test one is "simple." It is as simple as playing "Frère Jacques," whereas the Grand Prix resembles more the "Mephisto waltz" from Liszt (a piece that frightens many a great pianist).

This is perfectly right but, unfortunately, training level test one consists in playing "Frère Jacques" on a piano which is not tuned! Now, if you let me "tune" the piano (through lightness, hence balance), I probably will be capable of starting directly with a sonata of Mozart.

I have said that any average - but healthy - horse can perform someday some High School movements. What about the riders?

The answer to this question is theirs.

You perhaps think that you need a teacher. Now this can be taken care of, since you have not one, but *two* teachers at hand - your horse first, and...yourself, to boot.

If you abide carefully - *religiously* - by the philosophy exposed in this manual, you will progress...no doubt of that. And your horse - your best teacher - will tell you what he would like you to teach him. It is as simple as that.

Now, here is a short list of your possible enemies:

[124]

1) Lack in spirit of observation. Beaudant (1863-1948), the most prestigious of the Baucherists "second manner," would advocate, "observe, reflect." If the theory says one way, and your horse reacts another way, the theory is wrong and your horse is right. Perhaps, on second thought, you will find that the theory was somewhat right, but needed to be interpreted - adapted - to your horse.

2) Anthropomorphic reasonings, by which you try to interpret your horse's behavior as if it were of a man's. Don't call your horse a brat because he bucks when you canter left lead, and only with this lead. He is trying to explain to you that something hurts. Try and find what.

3) Defective seat. *This is the main snag.* If you want to ride in lightness, you must relinquish balancing from the reins *at all*. The nasty truth is that, if you are not or have never been capable of jumping a three-foot six-inch upright with your hands behind your back, you'd better forget about High School riding.

So, take your feet off the stirrups, cross the leathers over the horse's neck, and...have fun.

Be aware that your seat will *always* be unsatisfactory and *always* will have to be perfected.

4) Rudeness of hand, which betrays a lack of tact, politeness, and altogether of intelligence. You must constantly be literally torn between two apparently opposite requirements: the necessity of being efficient and the will to be soft. The will to apply possibly strong actions without "pulling." Think it over.

Last, but not least, remember that lightness does not consist in abandoning your horse beforehand and constantly; it consists in abandoning your horse *after having set him in a position or a balance which will allow him to perform the required movement.*